POETRY RE

SPRING 2000 VOLUME

EDITOR PETER FORB

ASSISTANT EDITOR STEPHEN

ADVERTISING LISA ROBERTS

CONTENTS

All illustrations by Gerald Mangan, except the BIFF on p43

Seeking New Writers

New Writing 10, an anthology of new writing will be edited by Penelope Lively and George Szirtes and published in May 2001 by Picador and the British Council in association with Arts Council of England. Some of the contents of the anthology are commissioned, but submissions (short stories, extracts from novels, poetry and non-fiction) are invited from authors or their agents for consideration. Priority will given to writers of British or Commonwealth nationality and to work that illuminates and illustrates British life and literature today.

The work must be unpublished and the authors should be willing to give the British Council world rights in all languages for the year following publication (the copyright remains with the author). There is no limit on the length of the pieces, but constraints of space mean that longer items will stand less chance of acceptance. Submission should be sent in duplicate, clearly typed for photocopying purposes, double-spaced and page numbered (with stamped addressed envelope for return if not used) to:

**New Writing, Literature Department,
The British Council, 11 Portland Place,
London W1N 4EJ**

POETRY REVIEW
SUBSCRIPTIONS
Four issues including postage:

UK individuals £27
Overseas individuals £35
(all overseas delivery is by airmail)
USA individuals $56

Libraries, schools and institutions:
UK £35
Overseas £42
USA $66

Single issue £6.95 + 50p p&p (UK)

Sterling and US dollar payments only. Eurocheques, Visa and Mastercard payments are acceptable.

Bookshop distribution:
Signature
Telephone 0161 834 8767

Design by Philip Lewis
Cover by Stephen Troussé.
Image courtesy gettyone Stone

Typeset by Poetry Review.

Printed by Grillford Ltd at
26 Peverel Drive, Bletchley,
Milton Keynes MK1 1QZ
Telephone: 01908 644123

POETRY REVIEW is the magazine of the Poetry Society. It is published quarterly and issued free to members of the Poetry Society. Poetry Review considers submissions from non-members and members alike. To ensure reply submissions must be accompanied by an SAE or adequate International Reply coupons: Poetry Review accepts no responsibility for contributions that are not reply paid.

Founded 24 February 1909
Charity Commissioners No: 303334
© 2000

EDITORIAL AND BUSINESS ADDRESS:
22 BETTERTON STREET, LONDON WC2H 9BU

telephone   0171 420 9880   fax 0171 240 4818
email   poetrysoc@dial.pipex.com   ISBN 1 900771 20 9
website   http://www.poetrysoc.com   ISSN 0032 2156

The Poetry Society
is supported by
BT

POETRY PLACES

by Peter Forbes

WHO KNOWS WHEN the first poet-in-residence was appointed? Perhaps it was Auden with the GPO Film Unit in 1935? 'Night Mail' is certainly a model for the commissioned poem. From the 1950s on, the idea of poets in residence started to take hold, with positions such as the Gregory Fellowship at Leeds University which brought poets like James Kirkup, John Heath-Stubbs, Peter Redgrove and Jon Silkin to Leeds and was so influential in the poetic apprenticeship of Tony Harrison, Wole Soyinka and James Simmons, amongst others. Some residencies, like this one, and the long-running Northern Arts Fellowship at Durham and Newcastle Universities (Tony Harrison, Anne Stevenson, Carol Rumens, Sean O'Brien, Bill Herbert, Jo Shapcott and many more) have acquired considerable prestige.

But the arrival of Poetry Places in 1998 with £150,000 from the National Lottery's Arts for Everyone Scheme clearly marked the arrival of a new paradigm. The scheme was the brainchild of Poetry Society Director Chris Meade, now Director of Book Trust after six years at the Society, which dramatically changed its profile. It was one of a series of initiatives that have increased the infrastructure for poetry. Most poetry residencies are relatively low-key, engaging and energizing the local poetry community but, besides its local impact, Poetry Places has had huge publicity and has entered the national consciousness, even if only at the level of the BIFF cartoon, with the traditional hi-falutin' notion of poetry continually colliding with the prosaic in supermarket check-outs, Northern Spirit trains, fish-and-chip shops and corporate lobby situations.

On one level, Poetry Places has complemented all the other swirling movements on the public face of poetry in recent years, generating spools of column inches to slot in between the Heaney and Hughes best-sellers, National Poetry Day, the Nation's Favourite anthologies, and Andrew Motion's latest poem, and providing virtually wall-to-wall media coverage. Reading the cuttings file, it is notable how many of the stories are written to

formula: wacky poet in prosaic location: what an inherently interesting situation! There is relatively little attention paid to the work produced by the placements. In a sense, the publicity *is* the point of Poetry Places, and if interest is fanned in the location and the poet produces a clutch of good poems as a result, that's a bonus.

Poetry Places is more or less over, with a few residencies still in place. The range of poets and locations is remarkable. No doubt poets' work stemming from the placements will continue to emerge for a while but it seemed a good time to look beyond those repetitive press reports and see what has been achieved. One important gain seems to be the enthusiasm for poetry that now exists in many large organizations such as British Telecom, Royal Mail, The BBC, and Marks and Spencer (the pioneering role of Poems on the Underground should not be forgotten here). Perhaps it was always there and simply needed Poetry Places to flush it out.

At its most serious level, Poetry Places is part of a movement that emphasizes the natural role poems play in life, including working life. *Poetry Review*'s 'The Secret Life of Poems' (Spring 1997) made a strong case for this, as does Daisy Goodwin's current anthology *101 Poems That Could Save Your Life* (Harper Collins). The strange amalgam of vestigial respect, actual indifference, fear and disdain that characterized many people's reaction to poetry for so long is yielding to a more natural acceptance. There is some way to go before people are going to feel as free to comment on a poem, for good or ill, as they do about film or music, but progress has been made.

Poetry Places was administered in its first few months by Helen Swords and latterly by Christina Patterson and Morag McRae, who have helped considerably in compiling this issue. The angles on the project, though, are entirely *Poetry Review*'s. In a satisfying closure rarely seen in arts bodies, the completion of Poetry Places led on to Christina Patterson becoming Director of the Poetry Society in mid-March. Another key poetry place secured.

New Take on the Times

CAROL RUMENS ON SIMON ARMITAGE'S POEM FOR THE DOME

SIMON ARMITAGE

Killing Time

Faber, £6.99

ISBN 0 571 20360 4

WHEN SIMON ARMITAGE and Glyn Maxwell were commissioned to "roll their own" *Letters from Iceland*, the result was the rather wonderful blend, *Moon Country*. What might have been mere imitation of the Auden-MacNeice project sparked the two into their own bold, mixed-media inventiveness. With *Killing Time*, Armitage again pays homage to a "'thirties" model. The nine long cantos that form the scaffolding of his end-of-millennium epic imitate MacNeice's *Autumn Journal* both in prosodic structure and panoramic ambition. For Armitage, unfortunately, the form represents the dilution of his protean imagination rather than its reinforcement.

Hedging his bets, perhaps, Armitage scatters a number of single quatrains among the cantos, and includes a couple of excursions into his more characteristic trimeter stanzas. Thus the prologic opening:

> There's a new freak in the ape-house,
> some monkey gone wrong,
> loudspeakers for earlugs,
> a microphone tongue…

Here – and at other points in the narrative – the poet satirises or demonises his original medium, TV, a gesture that added a nice subversive thrust to the broadcast script. On the page, however, the satiric impulse looks less urgent: any real poem, by its very nature, mocks TV stereotype-speak, whereas the absorption of such clichés into a poetic text, however intentional, tends to reduce the poetry. The habit of beginning cantos with the news-bulletin link, "Meanwhile", for instance, disadvantages them from the outset. It seems an easy substitute for the art of splicing the end of one canto with the beginning of the next, an art MacNeice had at his fingertips.

Like his mentor, Armitage is very good at reporting on the modern world in all its variety and freakishness, and he goes farther (our world, after all, is even more crazy than MacNeice's) in pursuing the freaks into the fantastical. The "Christmas" canto, probably his best, gathers and integrates a wealth of brilliant public and private detail, from the Tango Orange ads on Oxford Street to the child's homemade (Blue Peter-inspired?) manger where "Christ was a painted clothes-peg / in an After Eight box". Going on to explore, via the shift of "the bright star over the Middle East" into "cruise missile burn", a surreal, telly-visionary elision of battlefield and golf-course, the poem could have ended on its crisp comment about well-dressed prime-ministers mimicking well-shod presidents. But, as elsewhere, the poet has technical and philosophical troubles with closure, and, aspiring to a moral, lapses into some inconclusive banality:

Armitage's dilemma reflects our cultural confusions.

A genuinely populist and didactic poet, he is boxed in by a medium whose only alternative to relativism and cynicism seems to be a kind of easy-listening sentimentality.

> And there are always at least two sides to every story
> but when two sides say they are trying
> to do what must be done for the best in the eyes of
> their god
> they could both be lying.

Yes, but, on the other hand, they could both be telling the truth, as they see it, which is why such situations are so horribly hard to solve, viz. "the heavy pillow-case of peace in Ireland". Although the poem eventually succeeds in getting some kind of a "take" on all the odds and ends observed, its final war-haunted premonition feels too MacNeicean, too September 1939-ish, to ring true for other times, other wars: "and the thing we were told / was a thing of the past is coming up once more like the dawn, / and it is dark, and it is cold".

Armitage's dilemma reflects our cultural confusions. A genuinely populist and didactic poet, he is boxed in by a medium whose only alternative to relativism and cynicism seems to be a kind of easy-listening sentimentality. His film revels in simple, romantic images of "if only" – a sky full of balloonists, schoolboys handing flowers to their classmates instead of riddling them with bullets. In an audio-visual medium, because the visual carries so much more authority than the verbal, the accompanying text tends to dissolve into the subliminal, and the poet really need do very little but kill time. As the dry, self-doubting refrain, "we could do worse". comes round yet again, the viewer, lulled and pleasured by the sight of a sky gracefully raining balloonists, merely thinks, "Yes, sure". For the reader, though, it's more a matter of "so what?" Such extended journalistic conceits as the "flower-boys" narrative soon become embarrassing. Morality isn't that simple, and poetry knows it, if journalism does not.

Sometimes it seems as if a new kind of disposable poem is on offer. Compressing into literal images the Biblical notion of a thousand years being, in the Lord's sight, but a passing day, Armitage lets rip with a tumult of anachronistic celebrity snapshots: "Hitler on *Oprah*, / Stalin on *Esther,* Attila the Hun on *Celebrity Squares* / Pope John Paul / being Pope John Paul being Pope John Paul", etc. And my favourite: "Bill Gates fitting a window, / cutting his hand on a leading edge of bullet-proof glass". This is a poem you can run your eye over, skipping the bits that don't grab you. And it ends by saying much the same as it said at the beginning – so you can skip the conclusion, too.

The short poems generally work best: there's a powerful, imagistic one about the Ladbrook Grove train-crash, for example – or try the following quatrain for the way in which, nearly saying the obvious, it says something fresh:

> This season, luggage containing terrible thoughts
> was left in Brixton, Soho and Brick Lane,
> the kind which scatters the baggage of one man's
> mind
> into the public's brain.

Armitage could have done worse than produce a sequence of such "shorts". But the glamour of a long poem was required: a dome-sized, thousand-liner for the Millennium, which, unlike the Dome, wouldn't scare off a mass audience, and might even win poetry some converts. I hope it did. *Killing Time*, as a film, was a brave, imaginative try at a near-impossible commission, achieving memorability when it invited "ordinary life" to complicate the major theme. (That the major theme was, in fact, time, came across far more punchily in the "real time" of a TV film.) I think it was David Hare who said "a bad play can be good theatre." *Killing Time*, an unremarkable poem, would have been better served by publication in its rightful format, as a screen-play.

FLEUR ADCOCK
KENSINGTON GARDENS

DROPPINGS

Poetry for the summer. It comes out blinking
from hibernation, sniffs at pollen and scents,
and agrees to trundle around with me, for as long
as the long days last, digesting what we discover
and now and then extruding a little package of words.

POETRY PLACEMENT

They suggest I hold court in the Queen's Temple
(hoping it doesn't smell of urine).
Too exposed, I say; no doors or windows.
We settle for a room by the Powder Store (1805):
where else should poets meet but in a magazine?

PETER PAN

What was the creepiest thing about him?
The callousness? The flitting with fairies?
The detachable shadow? No,
that feature that was most supposed to entrance you:
the "little pearls" of his never-shed milk-teeth.

THE FAIRIES' WINTER PALACE

Queen Caroline, I think, planted these chestnuts
with their spiralling ridged bark. In another world
Peter and his freaky friends claimed this hollow one,
capacious enough for several children, if they dare,
to stand inside, holding their breath. Don't try it!

*****

HERON

A seagull on every post but one;
on the nearest post a heron.
Is he asleep? Stuffed, nailed to his perch?
He hunches a scornful shoulder, droops
an eyelid. Find out, fish!

HANDFUL

Now that there are no sparrows
what I feel landing on my outstretched hand
with a light skitter of claws
to snatch up a peanut and whirl off
are the coloured substitutes: great tits, blue tits.

JAY

A crow in fancy dress
tricked out in pink and russet
with blue and black and white accessories
lurks in a tree, managing not to squawk
his confession: "I am not a nice bird".

*****

SANDY

A cold day, for July, by the Serpentine.
She brings us up to date on her melanoma:
some capillary involvement, this time.
Just here is where her grandparents first met.
She still hopes to finish her family history.

*****

AEGITHALOS CAUDATUS

Don't think I didn't see you in the apple-tree,
three of you, hanging out with the gang, your long tails
making the other tits look docked; and in the roses –
all that dangling upside-down work – feeding, I hope,
on aphids. Come any time. My garden's all yours.

*****

BIRTHDAY CARD

This Winifred Nicholson card for my mother's birthday,
because she loves Winifred Nicholson's work –
or did, when she had her wits. Now, if all that's forgotten,
she may at least perhaps like it, each new time
it strikes her: "That's nice... That's nice... That's nice".

POLYPECTOMY

"You need a bolster", said the nurse, strapping a roll
of gauze under my nose, when my dressings threatened
to bleed into my soup. I sat up in bed
insinuating the spoon under my bloody moustache
and crowing internally: after all that, real life.

BUTTERFLY FOOD

The Monarch caterpillars were crawling away,
having stripped bare the only plant they could fancy.
We raced to the Garden Centre for two more,
and decked them with stripy dazzlers – lucky to have hatched
in NZ and not in the GM USA.

CHECKING OUT

In my love affair with the natural world
I plan to call quits before it all turns sour:
before the last thrush or the last skylark,
departing, leaves us at each other's throats,
I intend to be bone-meal, scattered.

*****

GOODBYE

Goodbye, summer. Poetry goes to bed.
The scruffy blue tits by the Long Water are fed
for the last time from my palm – with cheese, not bread
(more sustaining). The chestnut blossoms are dead.
The gates close early. What wanted to be said is said.

The Price of Everything

PETER SANSOM ON POETRY AND BUSINESS

THERE'S A POPULAR belief that poetry and business don't and perhaps shouldn't mix. The present remarks, which began as a talk (that, appropriately, was cancelled due to lack of take-up), hope in a roundabout way to address this, or something similar. A business-man or -woman would make shorter work of it, wouldn't we say, time being money. But I like sorting things out in language – through language – and that means giving words their head: which is why I say "or something similar"; I'm not entirely clear what issues this piece will address. Almost two hundred years ago, Coleridge noticed that "language as it were thinks for us". And thank Christ for that, is my feeling, because thinking's beyond me. More recently, John Ash – taking a swipe at Heaney's early 'Digging' – said, "Did you think you could just pick up language and use it like a spade, the one you call a spade". Well, the notion is that in the real world that commerce represents, they say, "I don't care what you call it, just get that dug". And maybe they do. Also that sorting things out in language means the poet likes the sound of his or her own voice, which is generally the case and in this instance is certainly so.

> This is probably the first perceived difference between business and poetry, that business is rational, gets to the point, says what it means; and poetry, well, that makes it up as it goes along and – when the reader's slogged through it – what does it boil down to? "Isn't life short"

This is probably the first perceived difference between business and poetry, that business is rational, gets to the point, says what it means; and poetry, well, that makes it up as it goes along and – when the reader's slogged through it – what does it boil down to? "Isn't life short" or "She's buggered off and I do feel fed up". Business, this is to say, is utilitarian. The poet on the other hand is worse than useless. In a meeting in an office dedicated to M&S's ideas for the millennium, they expected some lateral input from their poet in residence. My head was empty except for that man's haircut, and the way the woman always looked over my shoulder or at the floor, and wondering if it was me or her, and then what it was they did all day and how much they got paid. Evidently their job was to be creative, even though they were part of the machinery of this giant of high street retailing. Me, I'm only creative in words on paper. Some poets assuredly are "creative". There's Paul Durcan, for instance, the man (as Sean O'Brien says) with the left-handed head, or John Agard, whom I've met just the once and whose life seems to be a poem. Or Ian McMillan. *Geraldine Monk*. Most, I think, are like me, and not poets at all, but people who sometimes write poems, and whose lives, for good or ill, are given over to making that sometimes possible. However that is, my point is that the millennial think-tank is only a very obvious example of creativity in the business-place. It goes without saying that creativity is everywhere in business, not just those certain areas – design for instance or new product-placement – that immediately come to mind. It's worth pointing out something equally obvious, that many poets are also businesspeople. In their day-jobs, or indeed as freelance writers. And that not all poets are as useless as I flippantly remarked just now.

That poets can be extremely useful in business – even if like me they're not very Paul Merton about it – is taken as read at the Poetry Society. I won't go on too long about my own area of interest, on which I *have* gone on elsewhere (the Poetry Society website, principally): the idea of staff writing together, and sharing their work. We did this at M&S – an ongoing workshop at Head Office, and one-off visits to stores around the country – and everyone found it more than simply useful (and a lot of fun). I have this theory that writing poems is as natural as dreaming and may serve a similar function (especially if you don't interpret what comes out of it); and as such the writing and the sharing of work might loosely come under the heading of staff development. Running workshops is not necessarily the job of a poet, but I think poems are uniquely valuable in this instance because they are built of language in a particularly manageable (short, self-contained) form. And I think poets are often better than non-poets as facilitators, because of their experience of and their own relationship to language, and the fact that they've developed strategies which work, though mainly in fact because, even if they've thought a lot about it, they're not quite sure how those strategies work.

At this juncture, just where I ought to be detailing the benefits of poetry in the workplace, and perhaps trying to do more than merely assert that businesspeople are people and, despite some evidence to the contrary, so are poets (so that what we're dealing with here is really only a problem of naming, and the prejudices that come along with certain habits of naming) – just at this point, I want to turn in a slightly different direction. I want to talk about poets. First of all John Keats, a man who – as the *Letters* attest – might in a way have done anything, including being a successful businessman. And this despite the fact that the only awkward, not to say gauche, letter he seems ever to have written was to his publisher, for what after all was an advance but which seemed to him more of a hand-out – being an advance against sales which were unlikely to happen. I thought it would be interesting to discuss a statement of his, made in a letter, that "Everything is worth, as tradesmen say, what it will fetch".

Keats's truism plays on the fact that his reader will know it isn't true, and that it is. Also on the quite natural prejudice we have against tradesmen. They are selling us something and it's irrelevant to them if we need or even want it, so long as we will buy and they have their living, which is profit. It's irrelevant to them actually what their percentage comes from, the ode 'To Autumn' or one of the hats Keats's guardian thought he should go into making. Hang on though. When we write poems, isn't it irrelevant to us too if anyone needs them? It must surely be irrelevant to us whether anyone wants them. The difference is of course that we write poems for their own sake, and it's the selling that's irrelevant to us. If we write primarily to sell, to exploit a niche or supply a demand, the poems will be synthetic, factitious, dead. (I'll come back to this.)

There's snobbery in Keats's statement too, isn't there: "Everything is worth, as tradesmen say...". What do tradesmen know about art? And what, as a matter of historical fact, did Keats's poems "fetch" during his short lifetime? Keats knew his worth, "I

think I shall be among the English Poets" – but also how the market worked – "after my death".

We like this, don't we, this outrage against an age so dim it made the poet feel his name was writ in water, an error we would not make ourselves, and which inevitably we do, and are doing now. Or if not Keats, who died before he had time to earn the audience he must surely have found, we might ask for instance who the present day John Clare is. We might ask why it is we persist in buying the equivalent of those later Wordworth poems that frankly stink, instead of shelling out a subscription to get *The Midsummer Cushion*, or at least some more general selection of Clare's, into the book-sellers. Well, to do that, to appreciate that contemporary Clare, we would have (as Randall Jarrell would say) to be born again. There are literature panels, awards that recognize and foster talent – but even supposing they choose right, they can't make us read those poets. They can't foster a readership, though they may let us know the poet exists, and the poet may exist a little longer for the money they bring. Let me say here and now that I think cash awards are wonderful and personally I couldn't get enough of the things, though I know not everyone favours them. There's an essay by Humphrey House for instance that argues Coleridge's tragedy was the annuity from Josiah Wedgewood, when what he needed was the discipline of a job. What Humphrey House – you can't say that name too often – means, I suppose, is that Coleridge lacked self-discipline, wasn't organised, wasn't businessman enough, and being given money for nothing (for writing!) encouraged a sitting-on-his-arse proclivity. Fair to say though that Coleridge wrote considerably more than Humphrey House: the output of his various ventures, as we know, was phenomenal. Nevertheless, let's contrast not Humphrey House, about whom I know nothing except the name, but instead the Laureate Southey, about whom I know hardly much more, finding his verse either infuriating or soporific; sometimes, oddly, both. Robert Southey who worked so hard, often on Coleridge's behalf, and so efficiently and seemed able to do everything except write poems. He was serious and determined, and humble before the craft he mastered over a lifetime, and his writing brought pleasure to tens of thousands. Coleridge, it seems, fretted over the fact that, however he tried, he was not Southey; though Coleridge's tragedy actually was that he met Wordsworth, his opposite in temperament, and submitted to him. However that is, Coleridge was, to borrow a phrase of Simon Armitage's, "all voltage, no current", and yet, on strength of a handful of poems in a hardback *Collected* like a halfbrick, there he is "among the English Poets", Southey or no.

You might wonder where I'm heading with this. Me too. "A little knowledge is an English degree", as the saying is. But I think the drift of this is that poetry is in part a business, from which people sometimes make a living, and we've a tendency to think that in the free-market of culture you either do it so it sells – or earns you awards and prizes – or you do something else, like write a play (from which Coleridge earned more money than he ever did in fact from his verse) or journalism or run workshops, or work in a plastic mouldings factory, like Geoff Hattersley, one of the best and potentially best-selling poets around just now. It amazes me he's not on the telly or at least booked up months ahead on the readings circuit, a whole business in itself. "Fame burst like a meteor" on John Clare before the bottom fell out of the peasant-poet market. In his late "mad" poems, he counterfeited Byron – the ottava rima of a ventriloquist's dummy that has found its own voice: funny, satirical, beautiful and chilling – from our perspective – in their need for recognition. Clare who had already written better than Byron, poems that would wait till 1979 to see the light of day, and who, even then, even now, has more champions than readers and rarely merits a place in University modules or more than a couple of pages in anthologies, a vicious circle that distorts his achievement and excludes his best work from the canon.

This leads to Byron himself. He famously woke to find himself famous and soon rich for poems nobody reads nowadays. Later he held out for some extraordinary figure for the opening cantos of *Don Juan*. Not that he compromised his artistic integrity for the sake of a bestseller, declining forcefully to make changes, some of which Murray, fearing prosecution even more than his lordship's ire, made anyway. I don't have to tell you that, notwithstanding the exceptions which prove the rule – *Birthday Letters*, for instance – poetry as a business has changed since Byron's day. Though *Birthday Letters* deserves them, the reason for its sales has little to do with poetry *per se* as Byron's did.

This brings to mind the students on my course, usually young women, usually rather aggressive, who sometimes say they want to write about

Murray Lachlan Young, himself not a little Byronic. It's mainly the charismatic performance (they bring in a video) that appeals to them, and it's easy to see what they mean (and I don't *just* mean I wouldn't kick him out of bed either), though many are genuinely engaged by the verse on the page. Michael Schmidt, apparently, managed to tell M. L. Young, with ungainsayable charm – on air and to his face – that actually his poems were doggerel. It is hard to show Young's shortcomings to students without blunting their enthusiasm, and it's actually unnecessary, since his strengths are there to be learned from too and moreover mirror those in other writers whose success doesn't depend so much on the delivery. What is most difficult is evading the kind of timewasting debate people tire of rapidly apropos the pop poets (where often mediocre but dull poems were seen as preferable for the seminar room). "What it will fetch" then comes up hard against the dictum – following the Birdy Dance or sales of the *Sun* – that "Popular is Bad".

We distrust "palpable designs", as Keats says, but poetry may be a product placed in the market and still succeed as art. May still, I mean, avoid being what I called "factitious". For all those bands – Soft Machine were my favourite – blatantly ignoring commercial pressures to pursue their muse there's no doubting Lennon and McCartney's genius, and this partly because of rather than despite their attitude. According to a recent *Grimsby Evening News* ("Quotable Quotes" section), they'd generally sit down and say "Let's write another swimming pool". (What did they do with all those pools?) The two best poets of my generation are also the most popular.

Among the top twenty greats of the century, however – hovering round the top ten in my chart, in fact – is a poet hardly anybody has heard of, largely because he wasn't a businessman about it, his job being merely to write the poems, and his poems never quite suiting the market. This is a man called Stanley Cook, who published only with what's called "the small presses": those outfits who do it – as actually all poetry publishers do – from commitment or, if you'll forgive the expression, from love, and who can't afford to do much in the way of marketing, the business side of publishing. I mustn't get started on poetry publishing. If Eliot thought writing poems was "a mug's game", what does that make the publisher? As small businesses go, poetry publishing would have John Harvey Jones sucking his teeth.

JOHN MOLE
THE KNOWLEDGE

I loved you once (he said) but lost my bearings
somewhere between Brent Cross and Regent Street.
Her's was not the dress that you'd been wearing.
A different dish and good enough to eat.

She thumbed me down. I knew I was a gonner.
I felt the cab stretch to a limousine.
She belted up and sat there like Madonna.
So was this Tinsel Town or Palmers Green?

I crashed the lights, my heart a speeding arrow.
I wandered in a cloud from lane to lane.
With you the way ahead seemed straight and narrow
now that I'd started dreaming once again.

I turned the meter off. She saw me do it.
Neither of us cared to count the cost.
This was my Waterloo. She knew it.
The more she smiled, the deeper I was lost.

I loved you, yes, and we were good together,
always planned the route that we would take,
but now it really doesn't matter whether
here or there is right or a mistake.

I thought I had love's A-Z all sorted,
every twist and turn from grid to grid,
until the day she hailed my cab and caught it,
making The Knowledge change to what we did.

Written, as part of Poet in the City, for *Call Sign*, the in-house magazine
for London's Black Cab Drivers, and published in the issue for September 1999.

Footsie Wootsie

JOHN MOLE ON THE POET IN THE CITY SCHEME

AS A PLACEMENT, Poet in the City is nothing if not business-like, and as the son and grandson of chartered accountants I approve of that. Since its launch, a year ago, at a glittering event in the atrium of Clifford Chance and in the presence of its patron Wendy Cope, an energetic steering committee – with support from the Poetry Society and inspired by the enthusiasm of its initiator Rosamund Smith of Bates, Wells and Braithwaite – has set up a range of activities in businesses, schools, theatres and even on the steps of the Royal Exchange which have sought to create a community of poetry within the Square Mile. As the City of London's first official poet in residence, along with Eva Salzman, Jane Duran and Adisa, my brief has been to put myself about a bit, be there, see what happens, hear its music and make poetry while the glass-empire dazzles and the gold-leaf shines.

Initially, while the project was getting started, all the stereotypes came home to roost. They were encouraged, not least, by a sceptical press-coverage only too delighted to pick up on my (perhaps ill-advised) observation that Robert Graves once responded to a business man who was urging him to write a best-seller, rather than incomprehensible – to him – poems, by assuring him that "if there's no money in poetry, neither is there poetry in money". Rapidly, this remark became attributed to me in several sardonic news items. So what was I up to, selling out to Mammon and following the advice of Tennyson's worldly Lincolnshire farmer by going where money so conspicuously was? At the first of what have since become extremely popular Drop-Ins, chaired by myself and hosted by firms participating in the project – more about these later – I was made

welcome but with what seemed to be a degree of cautious generosity. Writing afterwards, in an in-house broadsheet, one of its participants reported that "John Mole wears a lot of corduroy, which is obligatory if you are a poet and writes movingly, intelligently and beautifully about love, which I understand is optional". What I have since discovered is that the reporter is, himself, a talented poet with a remarkable knowledge of contemporary verse, much of which he can recite from memory. At first glance I might have mistaken him for a charming member of the resistance.

So much for the stereotypes on both sides of a supposed divide which I have rapidly come to realise does not exist. "My solicitors", as friends often refer to them, may well be engaged in activities which bring in more dosh than I shall ever see but when they gather to share what in so many cases is an informed enthusiasm for poetry and an eagerness to discover more, I am reminded of what Roy Fuller – himself "something in the city" – wrote in his memoir, *Spanner and Pen*, about joining a working party of the Law Society: "It may sound pi, but one was convinced afresh of the essential honourableness, even self-abnegation of the profession, to say nothing of the brainpower of its best members". At the risk of sounding equally pi, even sentimental, I have become similarly convinced, not afresh but for the first time.

Perhaps I can best give some idea of the range and ambition of Poet in the City's activities by revisiting my itinerary for last year's National Poetry Day. It began with an appearance on Radio 5's early morning programme *Wake up to Money*. The project's press-release had included a short site-specific poem of mine, 'Whatever', written to be read at the Royal Exchange later in the day. It had attracted the programme's attention so, sandwiched between a couple of items about the state of the market, I was invited to offer a preview and answer a few questions. Living as I do in St. Albans and, from experience, wary of the Thameslink connection, I settled for a wake-up call at 5.30 am. and then went down the line a quarter of an hour later – by telephone rather than rail. My placement has not required me to write to order – no obligatory odes to the mayoralty or versification of the FTSE – but it has been impossible to let certain occasions pass without offering some discreetly "official" response to them. National Poetry Day was one such.

By 7.30 I had arrived in London at the offices of Wilde Sapte in Fleet Place. Here, at a considerable height, surrounded by a panoramic view of the city and guests from a galaxy of leading law firms, I was to help host a Poetry Power Breakfast. Andrew Motion, recently ennobled, was in attendance and before things got under way, we were interviewed for Radio 4's *Today* programme, Andrew being asked about poetry at large, and myself, inevitably, about the muse and Mammon. Then, after coffee and croissants, everyone sat down to what looked like an AGM except that all the papers, books and laptops contained poems. As has happened at the evening, after-work Drop-Ins hosted by various firms – of which this was a more lavish early-morning version – every kind of poem was read, from doggerel to Donne, some by their own authors and some only just discovered in books provided for the occasion by the Barbican Library service. The sense of relish was palpable, an oasis of delight at the start of a business day. My own contribution, typical perhaps of the kind of oblique input I like to make to the project, was my poem 'Breakfast at Drumcliff' which took as its starting point W. B. Yeats' observation that, for the poet, "the bundle of incoherence that sits down to breakfast" becomes in his poem "something intended, complete".

It was, though, the noon and lunchtime events which really characterised the outreach rather than in-house aspects of the placement. Funding has been 50:50 City businesses and charitable trusts (including the Sir John Cass Foundation) and when, from the steps of the Royal Exchange, 500 balloons carrying the Poet in the City logo and with their own poems tied to them were released by children from the Sir John Cass Primary School, to the amazement of passers-by, this symbolised the important link with education. The mixed funding

has underpinned a genuine partnership between the business and non-business sector. Several City firms regularly send employees into schools to help children with their reading and, as an extension of this link, I and the project's "satellite" poets have worked in over 20 schools in Tower Hamlets, Hackney and Islington, spending five days in each. In several cases the children have produced booklets of their work, given performances, and had their poems displayed on the South Bank as part of a millennium project. At the Royal Exchange event, after poems had been read by the winner of a competition run for cab-drivers by Call Sign, a member of *The Big Issue* writers' group, Sir George Staple QC, Alan Howarth, children from Sir John Cass and myself, a small boy (waiting to release his balloon) looked up at the imposing pillars of the Exchange and asked me "Is that where you live?" Then, from this communal earthbound gathering everything went sky-high for the children before they crocodiled back to school and the adults moved on to The Bridewell Theatre. Here the Education and Administration Manager, Rebecca Manson Jones, had created a marvellous installation. Poems were hung from the glass atrium, the lighting rig and wrought-iron balconies while Eva Salzman, Adisa and I presided over an informal drop-in where many City workers brought in their own poems to read. Rosamund Smith's declared aim – that we should all "celebrate with teachers, children and the wider community the diversity of poetic voices in the Square Mile" – had certainly been recognised.

Given more space I could say more: about the recording of one Drop-In on the theme of "laughter and death" by Radio 4's *Law in Action* and an account of another on "sport" by Michael Bywater in his *Independent on Sunday* column, about the project's involvement with BBC 2's series on the River Thames, about plans for further events if the funding can be found (including an extension of the workshops we have piloted) and the informal poetry circle set up at Lovell White Durrant to exchange poems by email. Little did I think, when I gave up teaching for the freelance life, that I should be spending so much, and such an enjoyable, time as a City worker. My father and grandfather would have approved, and have probably told me that it is never too late. Moreover I have learnt plenty, not least about the poetry of Wallace Stevens from a young solicitor who knows more about it than many poets of my acquaintance. A good placement cuts both ways.

ADAM TAYLOR
MY ENEMY

*The portrait painter Ingres was a perfectionist. One
painting, of a Mme Moitissier, took him 12 years. "My
enemy", he called it. He had to repaint her dress three
times because the existing one kept going out fashion.*

For hour after hour
While she sat in that chair
He assessed the effect
Of the light on her hair

He weighed up dimensions
Of height, depth and space
And how they informed
The contours of her face

During the series
Of preparatory sessions
Mademoiselle tried
A range of expressions

Seriously haughty
Yet somehow mysterious
Impish and naughty
With a dash of imperious

After some months
Of toil and trial
He decided to go for
The enigmatic smile

*   *   *   *   *

He dabbed and he daubed
With pigments and dyes
And slowly the painting
Materialised

Brimming with subtle
Yet pointed motifs
Later much copied
In Al Fresco's reliefs

Two little old men
And two larger old ladies
Playing bridge on the bridge
On the ferry to Hades

In their wake rose an oyster
Seated inside, the pearl
This embodiment of
The essence of girl

A reincarnation
Of divine Aphrodite
Barely attired
In a gossamer nightie

Her youth would stay frozen
Pale and sublime
Despite the relentless
Dripping of time

Those period features
Delicately chiselled
Would never be crinkled
Or jaded or grizzled

*   *   *   *   *

They came from afar
To the unveiling party
The creme de la creme
Of French literati

Anxious to see
The masterful oeuvre
Before it was carted
Off to the Louvre

One of those present
Was Toulouse Lautrec
He wasn't invited
He'd showed up on spec

In the midst of the throng
Stood mademoiselle
Having just lately
Emerged from her shell

Indifferent to
The froing and toing
The sighs and the gasps
The aahing and oohing

So they asked her, please tell us
Don't you like what you see?
She said, it really isn't
A good one of me

So the painter went home
And opened a beer
Then cut off his ear

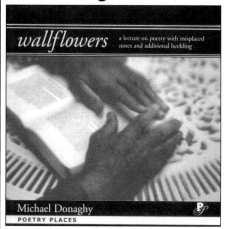

Poetry in the Pricking

PATIENCE AGBABI ON TATTOO POETRY

BEFORE LEAVING HOME this morning, I took a long, hard look at my back in the bathroom mirror. An hour later, sitting in Flamin' Eight tattoo and piercing studio, I winced as the vibrating needle drilled blue-black ink into my right shoulder blade. In two hours time, my entire back was transformed except for a blank space in the small of it, just enough room for a haiku...

I used to believe getting published was the ultimate poetic commitment. From the signing of the contract to the book launch, it meant words written in stone. For that edition at least, you had to live with that dodgy line, that irritating typo or that poem you'd grown to detest. My poetry placement in a tattoo and piercing studio has put all that into razor-sharp perspective.

My primary objective for the fifteen days was to create poems to be tattooed onto the skin although I had no idea whether anyone was brave enough to go through with it. A couple of friends had shown some interest but we hadn't discussed it seriously and I remained unconvinced. I toyed with the idea of advertising but was seriously daunted by the prospect of dealing with perverts who were more interested in pornography than poetry.

The day of reckoning came when Channel 5 approached me for their populist arts programme, *UK Raw*. They wanted to do a feature on my placement. I phoned my friend, Joelle Taylor, confirmed she was genuinely keen, and in less than an hour we'd arranged a tattooing date for the following week. It would be a serious collaboration between the tattoo artist, Naresh Bhana, the Channel 5 film crew, a couple of young, female rappers, Joelle and me.

That week I had to write five poems including Joelle's since the programme makers wanted us in four different locations. I wrote one-minute poems for a fruit-and-veg stall in Dalston market, Aquarius hairdressers in Finsbury Park, Upper Street's Bierodrome and Holloway Road's Flamin' Eight. The latter was a cheeky villanelle addressed to Naresh, 'Happy Birthday Tattoo'.

Meanwhile, Joelle and I had some in-depth discussions about our poem. She was very specific about its contents: it had to mention angels to correspond with her existing tattoo; it should ideally embrace the concept of writing and / or creativity as Joelle herself's a writer; and, if possible, it should incorporate the word "R. A. W.", since Joelle's a fan of my rap poem.

I enjoy writing to order and thrive on the challenge of a deadline so I spent an intense seven days creating a poem a day. Surprisingly, Joelle's piece was the easiest to write. The whole process was inspiring and rather than agonizing over every word, I found myself writing three pieces from which she had to choose. At one stage I became obsessed with the word-made-flesh concept so two out of the three pieces reflected that. They were also haiku. However, I wasn't able to fit Joelle's multiple themes into seventeen syllables so the unanimous favourite ended up being a twenty-six syllable acrostic:

Rhythm is the symphony of angels
Angels are muses with wings
Wings elevate words into rhythm

I detest proofreading yet as soon as Naresh had designed the tattoo, in Vatican lettering, I was the first to check the spelling of "Rhythm". Of course, the more you read a word, the more it looks wrong so Joelle had to assure me after the fifth time that everything was fine.

As the needle pierced Joelle's upper arm, I felt a rush of adrenaline. The poem was my first true collaboration and it already had an audience. Like most poets, I initially write for myself but in this case I had also written for Joelle. Simultaneously, I felt responsible for and able to let go of my creation.

Having a tattoo is as much about the choosing of the image, trust in the tattoo artist and the end result as it is about the physical sensation of being tattooed. The pain's part of the proactive metamorphosis. The healing process involves shedding your old skin like a snake to make way for the new. I believe that when it comes to the skin, committing to words is more absolute than committing to an image. Visual artists may disagree. But there's something irrevocable about making a literal statement on the body.

More recently, I've written a poem for another friend, Adrian Curwen. He's having the tattoo of a phoenix rising out of the small of his back. It was an interesting challenge working with an image and I eventually decided to have the words ascending with the flames or possibly even being the flames. The poem's a haiku, seventeen monosyllabic words intended to complement the phoenix:

Each time I set my past on fire I learn to sing a new kind of air

Although much of my time at Flamin' Eight has involved tattooed poems, I've also spent hours with the general public, collecting their stories and writing a series of tattoo poems which will be either displayed and/or performed at the end of my placement. Some highlights from my notes are as follows:

the tattooists' use of pigskin and / or live pigs to practise on; the mixed-race ex-member of the National Front with tattoos to prove it; and the man who joked, "A tattoo is for life / not just for Christmas".

My Flamin' Eight placement has enabled me to operate far beyond page and stage, allowing me to explore my ongoing obsession with the relationship between poetry and other art forms. People who wouldn't dream of picking up a poetry book have read the poem published on Joelle's upper arm, in the flesh, as well as in diverse magazines. The people who set foot in Flamin' Eight have had their experience enriched by reading, viewing and listening to poetry. I'll enjoy the reading on the final day of my placement, but my finest memory will surely be of staring at that Vatican "Rhythm" until the distinction between word and image became blurred.

PATIENCE AGBABI
IN INVISIBLE INK

Imagine the tip of my tongue's a full
Needle and your back's my canvas.

I'll tattoo you a secret if you promise
Never to read it out loud, break the spell
Vibrating its delicate, intimate Braille.
It'll remain locked in your skin. Even fierce
Sunlight won't betray my lemon juice.
In less than a fortnight the scar will heal
But we'll have words, you'll destroy my love
Letter by letter and I'll imagine somebody
Else touch-typing the keyboard of your spine,

Imagine our secret filed between skin and bone.
No. Don't say a word. My blind eye
Knows how to head my tongue, how to forgive.

Stanzaotherapy

by Mike Sharpe

FIONA SAMPSON

The Healing Word: a practical guide to poetry and personal development

The Poetry Society, £4.95
ISBN 1 900771 18 7

I REALLY CAN'T explain why it all seems to have happened in the last ten years or so – writers' groups in psychiatric day-hospitals, drop-in centres, residential homes, prisons. If such groups existed before, as most surely they did, they worked in comparative isolation, promoted locally by educationalists or innovative therapists. There was no-one taking an overview of their ways and means or documenting good-practice. It lacked, more than anything, a persuasive champion to put the case for creative-writing as a "worthwhile" even invaluable activity to potential sources of funding such as NHS Managers or Regional Arts Boards.

Fiona Sampson is one such champion with growing influence on the way writing in health-care is perceived. She's not alone, of course, but it's her experience as a practitioner that makes her work so trustworthy and informative. I think what's particularly significant is that she's an accomplished poet – and that gives a clue to the burgeoning success of what can only be described as a poetry and healing movement. Poets, who are not of necessity teachers or educationalists, have come to share their creativity in participatory workshops in the context of vulnerability or special needs. *The Healing Word* is Fiona Sampson's "practical guide to poetry and personal development activities". She was a member of the Poetry Society sub-committee that explored the concept of "poetry and healing" and her book was prepared as part of a Poetry Place residency with Salisbury Health Care NHS Trust.

Because the book is a Poetry Society initiative, I suppose its focus will inevitably be on the writing of poetry. "In the therapeutic context, someone who attends a session but writes prose, or nonsense, or nothing at all, is as much a participant as the person who turns out to have a wonderful feel for language". I'm sure that she doesn't mean to be merely tolerant of the prose writer or of the sense of achievement that comes with the simplest form of language discovery but I do think that the brief for poetry is unintentionally restrictive. That apart, I have nothing but admiration for all the guide's "hands-on" common-sense practicality.

As she stresses in her opening chapter, the Health Care Arts movement depends upon professional artists who "bring the arts into hospitals, hospice and day and primary care settings in order to humanise the whole delivery of clinical care". Writers work in the field not as trained "poetry-therapists" but in a "therapeutic context" where their involvement "adds value" to the work of therapists, clinicians and carers. She adds this crucial note: "Professional poetry isn't amateur psychology, shamanism or alchemy. Pretended expertise, especially when working with people made vulnerable by an event or illness, is a form of abuse".

This points to a problem not yet resolved – how can poets and writers become qualified for such work? She suggests three possibilities: shadow an experienced practitioner; work in hospital radio, the local hospice, or care work; undertake training. This last tells us where the movement has reached: it needs now a means of recording and co-ordinating good practice, of sharing experience and expertise, of giving new practitioners a body of understanding to underpin their first, tentative, ventures into working in a health-care context.

One such organisation is LAPIDUS, the Association for the Literary Arts and Personal Development of which Fiona Sampson was a founder-member. As she says in her book, the association is designed to be "a co-ordinating agency for individuals and initiatives in the field". Further, there's the possibility of real training with Dr Celia Hunt at the University of Sussex where her Post-Graduate Diploma in Creative Writing and Personal Development has been running since 1996. In 1998, Celia Hunt and Fiona Sampson worked together to edit a broad-spectrum of essays, *The Self on the Page*, which marked a major step forward in presenting an over-view of current practice. More than this, their contributors were exploring the theoretical basis of good practice, finding ways to "orientate the new field theoretically".

That there is so much happening and so much to be said, makes *The Healing Word* a very tightly compressed little book. A larger format would have made it less breathless, but I applaud the fact that it's been done and that its encouragement and advice is so soundly based.

PHILIP GROSS
AND POETRY?

The Galleries shopping centre, Bristol, October 1998

What are you selling? Nothing. Poetry?
Imagine a shaved monk, begging bowl
in cupped hands, offered up

like a gift, a free gift. Nothing, clear
as water, settling till it holds your face
and the faces that crowd in behind you

almost steady, or shivered minutely
by a heartbeat, someone's. Let it settle
deeper, till you see right through

to dented clay like the face of the moon,
and dust specks lifting, turning, as caught up
in their own world as me or you.

common place
public space
vox pop   can't stop   cut and paste

paperchase
human   race
litterpicking words   recycled waste

swirl down town
on the ambient sound
meet   greet   beat it   see you round

£ £ £ £ £ £ £ £ £ £ £ £ £ £

Umbrellas with ears,
fluorescent chairs,
"certain novelty items"
that "might cause offence"...
A child's voice: *Mummy? What's that for?*

Here where Little Bo-Peep
serves inflatable sheep
a poem pops up
out of nowhere,
a novelty. *Look*, it says, *There's more.*

£ £ £ £ £ £ £ £ £ £ £ £ £ £ £

A red E-type Jaguar
as glossy as a laquered nail.
      The surprised eyes of its headlights
      at finding itself here
massaged by two girls
in the company colours
      on overtime (next week, Swindon)
      with air hostess smiles.
If it had a voice (oh,
but it hasn't; its cylinders
      merely gleam)
      it might purr.

£ £ £ £ £ £ £ £ £ £ £ £ £ £ £

belt and brace
don't lose face
better buy a spare one   just in case

fashion bound
slimming down
you're better value   pound for pound

£ £ £ £ £ £ £ £ £ £ £ £ £ £ £

Oh. my love, my darling... – a wash
of harp, of dripping plinks, a fountain
fed by something else than gravity –
...oh, I'm longing for your touch...

coming round for the fifth time today,
a closed loop, but it's live: he's small,
wry, dark, eroded, like an old stone cherub;
she, sharp blonde and half his age,

is minder, front of house and sales.
We linger, lift our faces, close our eyes
as if to catch the cool of spray

though it's an old one – *such*
a long lonely time... Teabreak. We cluster
by the empty harp, and long to touch.

£ £ £ £ £ £ £ £ £ £ £ £ £ £ £

Going up, going down, two escalators
crossing in mid-air, for a moment
it was your face, half turned, and a man
beside you, how you softened to his touch

that stung me... then it wasn't you

of course: and that woman was anyone
and so was I, going up, going down
among window displays with knowing smiles
that say: here's what I wanted, always

wanted but until that moment never knew.

£ £ £ £ £ £ £ £ £ £ £ £ £ £ £

A smooth hum, as the lift
arrives; a hiss: the doors open
and we stand back,
making room

though there's nothing
in there, nothing's just the size
and shape of us, endlessly
consuming, endlessly consumed.

£ £ £ £ £ £ £ £ £ £ £ £ £ £ £

last chance astound
-ing gifts abound
huge reductions closing down

grave goods in a burial mound

we've lost all trace
of the inner space
of meeting minds   hearts touching base

and the cool embrace
pale skin black lace
where I meets I at the interface

on common ground
the lost and found
where a word meets a world re-verbed   re-nouned

where the costs-the-earth meets the reach-for-the-sky
where there's more to it all than meets the eye
and a poem is an advert for what money can't buy

like

   this

(the rarest thing of all in the public place)

a pregnant pause
a state of grace

£ £ £ £ £ £ £ £ £ £ £ £ £ £ £

(from words by Community Service Volunteers: Trees Of Time And Place scheme)

hush   listen   breathe
the swish   the silence
steamy summer heat
        the rich mulch smell
        past generations
        breathing in the peat
                whispers from creation
                written in the grain the gnarl
                of bark the flirt of leaves
                        the family foregathered
                        apprehensive – what now? –
                        like people   like people like trees

And Poetry...?

A breath, that's all
it is, a breath of other air

like the shade
of a bedouin tent, cool
drapes, a smell of coffee,

smoke, a certain
formality. Step in, barefoot,
out of desert glare

and speak, though till your eyes
become accustomed you can't see
who your host is; all you have

is your voice in the dark and maybe
there's no-one, nothing; maybe
there are all the others there.

JOHN WHITWORTH
CUDDLY WORDSMITH

Poetry Places makes poetry accessible to ordinary people.
Which must be good, mustn't it?

Try me. I'm poetry. I know you'll like me.
I'm now stuff po stuff. That stuff's what I do.
I'm poetry today. You'll *really* like me.
So come along, I'll show you what stuff's new.
Come in the lunch hour, find out what's hot,
The whatnot new stuff po stuff. Stop and try some.
I'm a now poet. I can spot what's what
Re now stuff new stuff po stuff. Come and buy some.
It's now. It's new. It's easy-peasy-poo,
Not that old hard stuff word stuff now-you-see
It-now-you-don't stuff. That stuff's not for you.
Try me. I'm soft. I'm stuffed. I'm poetry.
Worth an hour. I'll tell you over lunch.

Than you for listening, people. Thanks a bunch.

SOPHIE HANNAH

YOU WON'T FIND A BATH IN LEEDS

From the River Cam and the A14
To the Aire and the tall M1,
We left the place where home had been,
Still wondering what we'd done,
And we went to Yorkshire, undeterred
By the hearts we'd left down South
And we couldn't believe the words we heard
From the lettings agent's mouth.

He showed us a flat near an abbatoir
Then one where a man had died
Then one with nowhere to park our car
Then one with no bath inside.
With the undertone of cheering
Of a person who impedes,
He looked straight at us, sneering,
"You won't find a bath in Leeds".

"We have come to Leeds from Cambridge.
We have heard that Leeds is nice.
A bath is seen in Cambridge
As an integral device,
So don't tell me that a shower
Is sufficient to meet my needs",
I said. I received a glower
And, "You won't find a bath in Leeds".

He fingered a fraying curtain
And I said, "You can't be sure.
Some things in life are uncertain
And that's what hope is for.
One day I might meet Robert Redford
At Bristol Temple Meads.
I've found baths in Bracknell and Bedford
And I might find a bath in Leeds".

He replied with a refutation
Which served to increase our pain
But we didn't head for the station
Or run for a rescue train,

Though we felt like trampled flowers
Who'd been set upon by weeds.
We told him to stuff his showers
And we would find a bath in Leeds.

Some people are snide and scathing
And they try to undermine
Your favourite form of bathing
Or the way you write a line.
At night, while you're busy praying
That your every plan succeeds,
There are killjoys somewhere saying,
"You won't find a bath in Leeds".

A better definition
Might be reading all of Proust,
But the concept of ambition
Has been radically reduced.
While the London wits are burning
Their cash in the Groucho club,
In Yorkshire we're simply yearning
To locate an enamel tub.

I win, Mr Bath Bad Tidings.
I have not one bath but two.
En-suite in the sweet West Ridings
And no bloody thanks to you.
I may never run fast, or tower
Over Wimbledon's top seeds
Or hit sixes like David Gower
But I have found a bath in Leeds.

Poetry in the Post

PHILIP PARKER ON A YEAR OF COMMISSIONED POETRY

This is the Night Mail crossing the Border,
Bringing the cheque and the postal order.
(W. H. Auden, 'Night Mail')

THE 1930S IN particular was a golden era for creative Post Office commissioning. Leading graphic designers of the day were engaged in postage stamps and posters, and other media were being devised. In 1935, W. H. Auden worked for six months with the GPO Film Unit which at the time was busy inventing the documentary film genre. Auden composed a song for the film *Coal Face*, as well as the verse commentary for *Night Mail*, both of which featured collaborations with composer Benjamin Britten. *Night Mail* was the famous account of the nightly postal special from Euston to Glasgow. Less well-known is that Auden composed his verse to an edited version of the film, as a music composer would, even timing his spoken verse with a stop-watch so it fitted perfectly the shot on which it commented.

Such is the power of *Night Mail* that even after several decades it is fondly remembered. And after more than 60 years Royal Mail returns to poetry in earnest with a year of poetry commissions throughout 2000 accompanying its Millennium Stamps. In recent years Royal Mail has commissioned work from a range of poets: Steve Ellis composed a piece in response to the Rugby League stamps of 1995, and Benjamin Zephaniah composed a piece for the Notting Hill Carnival stamps in 1998.

Roger McGough's piece 'Timekeeper' accompanied a special set of stamps issued in December, the Millennium Moment, which was a prelude to a year of postal poetry. Throughout 2000, each of the 12 packs which accompany the Millennium Stamps features an especially-commissioned piece from a top British poet. The Poetry Society worked with Royal Mail to select a representative sample of British poets – each has been chosen to match their preoccupations and interests to the theme of the month's stamps. In January, Jo Shapcott's poem 'Night Flight from Muncaster' began the project in the 'Above and Beyond' pack. She is followed by 11 others, including one of the winners of last year's Simon Elvin Award for Young Poets. It is Royal Mail's most ambitious commissioning of creative writing ever. But why poetry?

The long history of The Post Office commissioning the leading creative practitioners (in visual arts, words and music) this century is continued with the Special Stamp programme (latterly the Millennium Stamp programme). Over the last few years, too, the literature accompanying the stamps (such as the packs) has explored different literary styles – from biography to children's writing – and commissioned leading writers, from Brian Aldiss to historian David Starkey, biographer Jenny Uglow and children's author Dick King-Smith. As the stamps have explored the concept of visual literacy, the words of the stamp programme have followed a complementary path of exploring written literacy, and poetry has played a part in this.

To commemorate the Millennium, poetry was considered a vibrant way of conveying the essential ideas about a subject in a minimalist format. In this way, poetry and stamp design are natural partners: distilling the essence of a concept down from a

Poets in Royal Mail millennium packs 2000

Jo Shapcott *Above and Beyond* (January)

John Agard *Fire and Light* (February)

Alice Oswald *Water and Coast* (March)

Tobias Hill *Life and Earth* (April)

John Cooper Clarke *Art and Craft* (May)

Moniza Alvi *People and Place* (June)

Michael Longley *Stone and Soil* (July)

Winner of Simon Elvin *Tree and Leaf* (August)

Lavinia Greenlaw *Mind and Matter* (September)

Ian McMillan *Body and Bone* (October)

David Hart *Spirit and Faith* (November)

Carol Ann Duffy *Sound and Vision* (December)

welter of ideas and facts. Since Royal Mail's business is that of communicating, and as the letters business of The Post Office, focusing on the written word in such a primary way is natural. Both stamps and poems can be thought of as miniature art forms, and poetry can explore issues in a way that other forms of literature cannot: they can be more emotive, direct, thoughtful – and can truly engage the reader.

The Year 2000 stamp programme was devised to be quite different from previous stamps. It is a photograph travelogue around the UK as it sees numerous millennium projects coming to fruition. The vision of 48 of these projects has been translated into 48 stamps issued in 12 sets. The titling of each set uses a coupling of words, such as "Fire and Light" or "Stone and Soil" to create a millennial sense of the theme being explored on the stamps, and to provide a poetic feel to the year. Poetry in the packs explores this concept further. The 12 packs will build into a contemporary anthology of stamp design and poetry. Additional poetry activities are also planned during the year.

There are historical reasons for championing poetry, too. Arguably, British poetry has a longer continuous history of excellence than any other in the world. British poets have been internationally recognised in a way that is only occasionally true of our painters, sculptors and composers. We are a nation of poets – from Shakespeare and even before him. And with the year 2000 also marking the anniversaries of the deaths of Chaucer (1400) and

Poet Laureates John Dryden (1700) and William Wordsworth (1850), it is fitting that the packs will feature some of the most stimulating poets at work in Britain today.

Poetry has been called "the new rock'n'roll". Whether or not this is true, it enjoys enormous popularity. Survey results show that at one time or another most people put pen to paper and try their hand at poetry. The Poetry Society's annual National Poetry Day is always well received, with the poll of the Nation's Favourite Poem receiving hundreds of thousands of votes. Today we can come across poetry in almost any location: in underground trains and on buildings, and poets in residence have worked in locations as diverse as London Zoo and Marks & Spencer. Last October, Salisbury became poetry city when the work of almost 100 poets was displayed around the town: in shop windows, on the cathedral and even tattooed on a volunteer. Jo Shapcott was one of the organisers of this project, which included Carol Ann Duffy's musings on the postal millennium which adorned envelopes. The tempo may be different from Auden's 'Night Mail', but the idea of the mail as messenger is as relevant, and timeless, as ever.

Postman, postman be as slow as you like
delivering this, your wobbling bike
barked down city streets, round country bends,
on your back a sack, bulging
with all our whispering, singing, yelling words
as the twentieth century ends.

MIMI KHALVATI
WRITING LETTERS

After chapel on Sundays we wrote letters.
Ruling pencil lines on airmails. Addresses
on front and back often bearing the same name,
same initial even, for in some countries
they don't bother to draw fine lines between
family members with an alphabet.

Those who remembered their first alphabet
covered the page in reams of squiggly letters
while those who didn't envied them. Between
them was the fine line of having addresses
that spelt home, home having the ring of countries
still warm on the tongue, still ringing with their name,

and having addresses gone cold as a name
no one could pronounce in an alphabet
with no *k-h*. Some of us left our countries
behind where we left our names. Wrote our letters
to figments of imagination: addresses
to darlings, dears, we tried to tell between,

guessing at norms, knowing the choice between
warmth and reserve would be made in the name
of loyalty. As we filled in addresses
off by heart, the heart drew an alphabet
of doors, squares, streets off streets, where children's letters
felt as foreign as ours from foreign countries.

Countries we revisited later; countries
we reclaimed, disowned again, caught between
two alphabets, the back and front of letters.
Streetnames change; change loyalties: a king's name
for a saint's. Even the heart's alphabet
needs realignment when the old addresses

sink under flyovers and new addresses
never make it into books where their countries
are taken as read. In an alphabet
of silence, dust, where the distance between
darling and dear is desert, where no name
is traced in the sand, no hand writes love letters,

none of my addresses can tell between
camp and home, neither of my countries name
this alphabet a cause for writing letters.

MATTHEW SWEENEY
FROG-TAMING

Any fool can learn to catch a frog –
the trick is to do it blindfolded,
lying there, in the wet grass,
listening for the hop and the croak.

And the real trick is to keep it alive,
not strangle it, or squeeze it dead –
that way you can take it home
and tame it, make it your pet.

But early on, keep the cat locked up.
Soon she'll get used to her odd sibling –
meanwhile put a bit of time into
picking a suitable name for a frog.

And research a frog's ideal diet,
also the best sleeping arrangement –
water somewhere nearby, of course,
and plenty of air, plenty of air.

Be sure to play the frog the right music
so it can learn hopping tricks –
ones it can reproduce on the cleared table
when you have dinner-guests around,

while you find your blindfold and put it on,
holding your hands out and grasping
the air the frog has just vacated –
making it clear you're deliberately missing.

BERNARDINE EVARISTO
IN MEMORANDA

*In 1996 remnants of an early human, a robust leg bone and two
teeth, 500,000 years old, were found at Boxgrove, West Sussex.*

I slip beyond consciousness, falling
through London's grey slabs, tubes
of electric coils, pipes of hard, leaded
water – I sink into rivers of effluvia,
layers of chalk, dark clays and down
into the lithosphere where plates shift
deeper still and subducted into miles
of tectonic crust, I am sucked towards
the hellish molten core,
and explode.

Cloud of dust and volcanic gas
made this planet, cells spawned fish,
green, mammal, primate – hominids
so far back we only find fragments now,
calcified in lime water stalagmite, tracks
fossilized under volcanic ash. 1972 –
Lucy's fifty-two bones discovered in Hadar,
Lucy in the Sky with Diamonds, Fab Four
harmonies filling Ethiopia's night sky,
at the wake, three million years, on.

Australopithecus africanus evolves
into australopithecus robustus, emerging
Homo species – found: Boxgrove Man,
half a million years waiting
for a post mortem, '*Of warm-adapted
African origin, six footer, in his twenties,
aggressive, predator-type, inarticulate,
immigrant sans passport, no doubt*' –
who first roamed this wild terrain
we call – England.

Poetry Tickets Please

IAN McMILLAN ON TRAINS

I'M WANDERING THROUGH the Shipley to Skipton train giving out my Northern Spirit Christmas card, as part of my job as Poet on the Trains. Some people gaze curiously at the card with its happy snowman and jolly verse. Some say "I've seen you on the telly". Some comment on the lateness of the train. I only get one refusal: it's a middle-aged lad out with his mam. They look as if they've been written by Alan Bennett. I proffer the card. "Don't take it, Jeffrey", she barks. He looks at me with tragedy in his eyes. I put it on the seat next to him. "Don't look at it, Jeffrey", she says, her lips as tight as a biro line. All in a day's work for the Poetry Placee!

I've only had one official Poetry Placement, with Northern Spirit, but I've been poet in residence all over the place, from the Co-op car park in Cambridge in 1983, via Age Concern in Leicester in 1987, to Barnsley Football Club (ongoing), and I'm sure that the idea of putting poets in places has helped to raise the profile of poetry to the happy state it s in today.

My job with Northern Spirit is perhaps a good example of what happens to a Poetry Placement and how it can take on a splendid and, well, poetic life of its own. Northern Spirit is sponsoring the Ilkley Literature Festival in a big way and it seemed like the obvious thing to do to have a Poetry Place. I'm fairly well-known in the Yorkshire area, mainly due to my appearances as Yorkshire Television's Investigative Poet, and I'm also known to be a non-driver and a fan of trains. The job was a ten-day one, and would involve going on the train with various groups including grammar-school kids, infants, and adults with learning disabilities, as well as doing poetry workshops with Northern Spirit staff and sitting on the trains on my own and writing. I wrote a performance poem for the launch day, mentioning as many Northern Spirit stations as I could think of (Wakefield Westgate / Wakefield Kirkgate / Bradford Forster Square / Train is rolling / Through the heavy / steaming Yorkshire Air, and so on) and the project was launched at Shipley station with a reading of *Night Mail* by the actor Barrie Rutter and me performing my station name poem on the train to Ilkley with lots of friends and supporters of the festival and the biggest media

scrum I've ever seen. I should have guessed, really, since my Barnsley FC job attracted a lot of attention, but this was definitely like being famous for half a day. I was on BBC, ITV, Sky News, World Service, the Jimmy Young Show, You and Yours and more local radio stations than I could count. Most of the interviews took place by telephone in the corner of a pizza house near the station. I read my station names poem over and over again. All the interviewers asked if I'd be reading the poems out to baffled commuters, and I said I might. None of the interviewers asked how long the job was for, and I'm sure they all assumed it was for life, or at least for five years. Over the next few days it carried on. I was interviewed on my local train station by Radio 3; a man from *The Independent* took my photo in a train on Barnsley station and the guard wouldn't wait and the poor snapper was hurtled to Wakefield; I was, gloriously, on *The Big Breakfast* reading poems out from a posh chair on Shipley station; I was on German Television and BBC1's Heaven and Earth; a letter was published in *The Independent* saying "If Ian McMillan is going to be popping up on trains reading poems, that's a good advert for women-only carriages"; I had to stay up late and read an Australian version of my station names poem on Australian Breakfast Radio, and a researcher tried to get me to go on a live TV debate, even though I was filming something else in Scotland that day, "This could make your career", he said. "I can't pay you anything but I can fly you there and back". Don't touch it, Jeffrey!

I realise that my experience isn't unusual, and that most of the Poetry Places have attracted similar attention; what worries me a little bit is that the attention has sometimes been seen as a little bit unsavoury, a little bit demeaning to poetry, as though appearing on *The Big Breakfast* or Australian radio might cause the precious jug that is poetry to fall to the floor and smash into a thousand pieces. Of course the opposite is true; the more publicity the Poetry Places get, the better. To others in this position I would say Enjoy; enjoy being the centre of attention for a few days, do all the silly things they ask you to (Would you just read that poem to those commuters again, from a different angle? Would you just hold that poetry book up and begin reading from it at the exact moment the guy blows his whistle to set the train off? Would you tell us what you think your poems have to appeal to older readers because our magazine is for older readers?) And remember that all this is good, or maybe very good, for poetry.

And what did I do in my ten days? Well, I spend a lot of my time on trains, and I find them powerful places for contemplation and for the creation of poetry; I also find them wonderfully communal places where, like it or not, you have to mix with your fellow human beings, and I wanted to share that with big gangs of kids and adults. So, I took a gang (or rather two gangs, one in the morning, one in the afternoon) of infants onto the train on a terrible wet and windy morning. I'd already performed to the whole school, setting up the idea of the journey we were going on, and me and the infants and the teachers and the helpers sat and gazed in wonder at the things we saw, the things we'd never normally get a chance to look at because we'd be too busy doing the Literacy Hour; ordinary things took on extraordinary significance as we looked at them: the discarded bicycle, the two men in flat caps walking side by side, the sodden washing hanging in the deserted garden. The guard joined in the fun and turned the lights off as we plunged into a tunnel. The excited screams were pure poetry, as far as I could see. And of course, being a Poetry Place, the day with the infants had to be recorded for the local paper; a nervous lad photographed me leading a group down the platform like an obese pied piper. Then back at school we made communal poems, made pictures, talked about what we'd seen and the journey, only a few miles through damp moorland, became an epic adventure. It was the same with the secondary school kids, and the Northern Spirit staff, as we sat in an office with paper and Danish Pastries, delightfully the same with the adults with learning disabilities; ordinary journeys, ordinary visions made extraordinary. Sounds like the roots of poetry to me!

The present round of Poetry Places has ended, but I feel passionately that they should carry on in some shape or form, and that they should get even more daring and unusual. Poetry Places everywhere? A true democratisation of the art? Go on, Jeffrey, pick it up!

TOBIAS HILL
THE LIGHTHOUSE KEEPER'S CAT

In 1895, a new species of wren was discovered on Stephen's Island, New Zealand. The Stephen's Island Wren was identified only from dead specimens: the last had been killed by the lighthouse keeper's cat.

All day it lies as if extinct,
coiled as an ammonite
at the foot of the spiral stairs;
or basks in the primacy of sunlight.

Only at night it brings him gifts.
The lighthouse keeper wakes
to the tick of ghost crabs
left for dead, or wrens so small

he almost misses them,
so warm he takes them for living,
the fishbone teeth
having held them so carefully.

Before he came to the island
he imagined the rocks,
the flotsam of wrecks,
and instead of these he found

the bright peoplings of birds.
The balance of hawk and gull
over green hills. Swifts wintering.
The hummingbirds greener than green.

He climbed the damp helix of stairs
to where the lamps on their axis
had grown solid with a weld of rust,
immobile in the salt air.

Nineteen days in the mending,
and only his cat
moving around the round room.
The animal turning and turning

like a warning of something happening
or yet to happen. Those first nights
he slept not knowing yet what he had done,
or what moved through the green and greener hills,

uncoiling under the lamp of the moon
to bring him back its small, delicate gifts.

JACKIE WILLS

HANKLEY

At weekends, or when evenings last
my mother puts us in the old grey Rover
with the dog and drives to Hankley.

In the pond, by the car park, fishermen
hunch under umbrellas big as tents,
nets slouched in the shallows, and summon

pike big enough to take a hand off.
The water never moves. This is the place
in the woods we walk away from.

The pond's too much like home.
On the common we struggle through sand
churned up by trucks. She warns us

to stay out of the heather, where lost flares
and cartridges hide, unexploded. We walk,
and talk more easily than in the house.

The sky opens us up and in summer
it's as if fire cracks in every stem,
burns in the sun on our necks

the prickly heat reddening my mother's hands,
in clumps of beaters, stacked like paddles
waiting for canoes, and a river to carry them.

Then it's gone. Leaving patches of charcoal,
maps of new territories scored into purple;
landmarks which will last a year at most.

There were Daleks here. We know
there are targets where soldiers lie low
on their stomachs and wait, like the pike.

From Texas to Northumberland

NICHOLAS BAUMFIELD ON COWBOY POETS IN RESIDENCE

IN AUTUMN LAST year Joel Nelson from Alpine, Texas, came to Rothbury, Northumberland to take part in the Poetry Society Poetry Places scheme. Joel Nelson is a rancher and stockman, but also a leading light in the revival of Cowboy Poetry in the Western states of America. Rothbury is a small market town in the Coquet valley in Northumberland – rural, remote, bordering on Scotland, very different in some ways from the plains of Montana but with much that matters in common.

Cowboy poetry dates back to the epic cattle trails of the 1800s when long, lonely hours were spent contemplating the landscape, the elements and nature itself

That strong and silent type –
The one you read about –
He's kinda forced to be that way
When the drive's all scattered out.

But he ll get downright eloquent
When the evening chuck's washed down,
And it's sunset in the cow camp,
With the crew gathered 'round.
(Joel Nelson 'Sundown in the cow camp')

Of course the work of ranch-hands, packers, fencers and horse-trainers has continued and in the mid 1980's working cowboys began to revive the recital and writing of poetry. Now huge annual gatherings of cowboy poets take place with audiences of thousands. One of the largest is at Elko, Nevada – if you visit the Western Folklife Centre website you can hear some of the events for yourself (www.westernfolklife.org).

In 1995 the Northern Poetry Library hosted a visit by four cowboy poets who were making the first ever tour of the UK. Rather than present them purely as exotic and large-than-life characters their show in Northumberland included two poets and a singer from the Border Shepherd tradition: Alan Wood, a retired sheep-shearer; Graham Dick, a shepherd and singer; and Andrew Miller, a poet, National Park Ranger and mainstay of the Coquetdale community. What emerged was a celebration of common ground and shared experience

of working on the land and with animals. The event was a success, not least with the visiting cowboy poets. In the following years all three Northumbrians were invited back to Elko together with Katrina Porteous, another Northumberland-based poet who was asked by the Western Folklife Centre to research the roots of cattle-droving poetry in the Northumberland hills.

The Poetry Places scheme provided a wonderful opportunity for putting a Cowboy poet into the special place that is Coquetdale. The aim was simply to encourage poetry: recital, writing, reading and listening to it. Mid-Northumberland Arts Group took the lead with help from Graeme Rigby, writer and enthusiast for tradition, Katrina Porteous and Andrew Miller. Joel Nelson was delighted to accept the invitation and he arrived at Newcastle airport on a fine autumn afternoon.

Joel Nelson proved to be a remarkable man. He is a very experienced horse-trainer and one of his first visits was to a horse breeder in Thropton. He got up onto a horse straightaway and cut a figure against the Simonside Hills, perfectly at ease, completely in control of his steed. His poetry displays the same composure. He is a man, also, of quiet but great charisma, infinitely courteous and gracious. At every public event he appeared in – the back room of the pub at Alwinton, the young farmers meeting in Thropton, the final show at Alnwick, he completely captivated his audience. His voice, of course, was pure Texan and he was recognisable in any crowd by his large black cowboy hat, which he never, ever takes off (except when eating at table). As an inspirational force for poetry he is incomparable.

Joel spent a month in Coquetdale meeting the farming families of the valley, visiting schools, attending marts and shows such as the Rochester show and the Rothbury Calf Sale, taking part in the numerous societies, clubs, groups and meets that make up the rich cultural life of the valley. Everywhere he went he started by exploring what was different and what was the same, and ended up with poetry. People who had never revealed their own writing brought it out for the first time, others who wrote or who recited (recital remains a vital part of the village shows and fairs in

Northumberland) delighted in sharing their verses; new poems were composed by some; others just listened to the poetry and revelled in it. The effects are still being felt.

In Thropton First School Joel talked about a friend of his called Henry Real Bird. The Year 3 children thought about new names for themselves which had an association with an animal: Jonathan Giddyabout, Andrea Tigger-Bounce, Sarah Hamster Sleep-All-Day. Then they wrote poems in which they had imaginary conversations with an animal. This is Daisy Lazarus' poem:

My name is Daisy Goatbirth.

I talk to the fox,
Fox, I hate it when you scoff my chickens.
You can come to my house
If you don't scoff my chickens.

The fox says:

I'd like to be your friend –
But I like your chickens better.

Joel hadn't worked much with young children before but they were spellbound by him, and there were many other striking poems written (as well as many young people intending becoming cowboys later).

As Joel was waiting in the airport cafe to leave a very small boy came up to him to say hello, his mother having ascertained that this was the cowboy poet they'd heard about. Joel bent down to speak to him but the boy had only one burning question: "Where's your horse?" Somehow it was a telling moment: two people brought together through poetry, a place and their connection with the natural world.

Paratextual Possibilities

by Roddy Lumsden

MICHAEL DONAGHY

Wallflowers: a lecture on poetry with misplaced notes and additional heckling

The Poetry Society, £4.95
ISBN 1 900771 14 4

YOU MAY RESPOND to Michael Donaghy's unusual Poetry Places designation – Creative Reader in Residence – with a quizzical look. After all, isn't it the place of a writer to do the task-work of creativity, the reader's part being to kick off shoes and settle deeper in the armchair? Donaghy's task was to shrug off his shopkeeper's overalls and come back out front to do some window-shopping. Part of the haul was this book, the text of a lecture he gave in London last year.

He begins by expressing his love of "wilfully eccentric...precepts" and conjures one of his own from a memory of a vision at a *ceilidh*. The tumult of the dancers had seemed to provide a visible embodiment of the music; the "scuffs and streaks their heels had made" providing a record or pediscript of their pleasures, "an enormous encoded page of poetry". In this scenario, the reader is akin to a wallflower, scared to dance or wishing to be asked.

Donaghy looks back to a time before readers, when an oral tradition arose from the need to memorise and pass on knowledge, hence mnemonics, rhyming and storytelling constructs: the mental "dance which only comes alive with the participation of an audience". As listener evolved into reader, the sing-song and the storyteller's tics were replaced by the paratextual possibilities of the page. Even before printing, monastic scribes would pepper the margins with musings and Greek chorus-style commentary. By the time of Coleridge (as Kevin Jackson shows in *Invisible Forms*, an excellent and accessible recent book on paratexts), the text was accompanied by a small orchestra of asides – marginalia, footnotes, acknowledgments, errata etc.

Yet still, like circling dogs, we retain traits which bond us to tradition. The reader's voice keeps its pact with the text, as Donaghy notes: "as you read... your breath and throat muscles are changing subtly in response". We are bound by expectations which arise from speech and poets exploit these, not least by playing them off against form to make a poem memorable or "memorisable".

The relationship of poet and reader is one of musical chairs. Donaghy suggests that a poet must imagine "oneself in the place of potential readers in order to anticipate one's effect" and adds to this the poet's ventriloquism: "sensitive readers give themselves up to the poet for the duration of the poem". But should we trust the reader; is there any integrity in the truism that "a poem is only as good as its reader"? In Donaghy's home town of New York, I once waited to view a Hopper painting while a crowd of small children offered amusing, unlikely interpretations of the scene to their teacher. They passed into the next room, as soon did I; the painting hung there non-plussed. With paint and print, the problem lies in our response to the artefact as opposed to the art. Maybe, for interaction, as opposed to response, we need to return to being listeners, in the context of a poetry reading, and to take the poet's arm and join in the reel.

Beyond the familiar roles of reader/listener, Donaghy brings up the subject of signed poetry composed by deaf poets. Watching a signed poem, whose transcribed text has seemed rather flat, Donaghy notes how much is lost in the translation (the bodily rhythm, the shifts of pace, the facial expression) and quotes Collingwood: "writing, in our always notative, can represent only a small part of the spoken sound... pitch and stress, tempo and rhythm, are almost entirely ignored..."

I can't fully agree with ideas discussed here by Donaghy on the "organic" origins of poetic forms. Studies indicate that poetic forms may have arisen from the introduction of "right-brain processes into left-brain activity of understanding language" and that an "auditory information 'buffer' of three seconds' worth of information" may be behind the units of language which make up poetry. He quotes, too, from theories linking the sonnet, the Golden Mean and the Fibonacci series. Yet if the sonnet did evolve from "innate ordering principles", wouldn't we now have sonnet equivalents in Swahili and Quechua?

The most striking among Donaghy's "eccentric precepts" is the idea of emblematic "transitional objects" offered by writer to reader – "in our unconscious desire to locate the presence of the poet...we try to animate the poem itself". This is often done through focus on detail – you may not empathise with Elizabeth Bishop's Crusoe, but you can almost grab at that knife she has him rely on. Donaghy leads us through poems by Harrison, Browning and others, analyzing the magic, giving away the secrets of the conjuror's tricks. *Wallflowers* is reeling full of charming, thought-churning ideas, swaying with mad facts and sudden tangents. Don't be shy now, Take a dance!

ILYSE KUSNETZ
ENGLISH HORN SOLO

(after Eugenio Montale)

The predatory wind that plays tonight
– a devil banging on a metal drum –
the long pipe of the aspen, and sweeps
the copper horizon
where light is streaming,
kite-tails in a roaring sky
(arrowing cirrus, lit realms
above us – exalted Eldorado's
doors ajar!), or
the sea that scale by scale
alters its colour,

and breaks a twisted horn of spume
across the broken underland;
the wind that is born and dies
as the world's hour dims –
if only it could play you too, tonight,
faulty instrument,
heart.

GRACE NICHOLS
THE GARDENER

(Paul Cezanne, 1906)

Sitting crossed-legged
under the roof of my hat
hour after hour

Hearing the leaves
of those brushstrokes
overlapping colours

The workings of greens
and browns and blues
the light over my shoulders

The patience of seed
the gesture of flowers –
my ten green fingers.

JOHN AGARD
REMEMBER THE SHIP

As citizen
of the English tongue

I say remember
the ship
in citizenship

for language
is the baggage
we bring –

a weight
of words to ground
and give us wing –

as millennial waters
beckon wide

and love's anchor
waiting to be cast

will the ghost of race
become the albatross
we shoot at our cost?

I'm here to navigate –
not flagellate
with a whip of the past

for is not each member
of the human race
a ship on two legs

charting life's tidal
rise and fall

as the ship
of the sun
unloads its light

and the ship
of night
its cargo of stars

again I say remember
the ship
in citizenship

and diversity
shall sound its trumpet
outside the bigot's wall

and citizenship shall be
a call
to kinship

that knows
no boundary
of skin

and the heart
offers its wide harbours
for Europe's new voyage

to begin

From The Guardian, January 17 1998

THE CLASSIC POEM

WRITTEN AS FAR back as 1979, Fleur Adcock's poem makes a significant stage in the evolving self-consciousness of poetry and is uncannily prescient of the era of mapping and placing we now inhabit. As the poem says: "Stones that have been so fervently described / surely retain some heat".

FLEUR ADCOCK
PROPOSAL FOR A SURVEY

Another poem about a Norfolk church,
a neolithic circle, Hadrian's Wall?
Histories and prehistories: indexes
and bibliographies can't list them all.
A map of Poets' England from the air
could show not only who and when but where.

Aerial photogrammetry's the thing,
using some form of infra-red technique.
Stones that have been so fervently described
surely retain some heat. They needn't speak:
the cunning camera ranging in its flight
will chart their higher temperatures as light.

We'll see the favoured regions all lit up –
the Thames a fiery vein, Cornwall a glow,
Tintagel like an incandescent stud,
most of East Anglia sparkling like Heathrow;
and Shropshire luminous among the best,
with Offa's Dyke in diamonds to the west.

The Lake District will be itself a lake
of patchy brilliance poured along the vales,
with somewhat lesser splashes to the east
across Northumbria and the Yorkshire dales.
Cities and churches, villages and lanes,
will gleam in sparks and streaks and radiant stains.

The lens, of course, will not discriminate
between the venerable and the new;
Stonehenge and Avebury may catch the eye
but Liverpool will have its aura too.
As well as Canterbury there'll be Leeds
and Hull criss-crossed with nets of glittering beads.

Nor will the cool machine be influenced
by literary fashion to reject
any on grounds of quality or taste:
intensity is all it will detect,
mapping in light, for better or for worse,
whatever has been written of in verse.

The dreariness of eighteenth-century odes
will not disqualify a crag, a park,
a country residence; nor will the rant
of satirists leave London in the dark.
All will shine forth. But limits there must be:
borders will not be crossed, nor will the sea.

Let Scotland, Wales and Ireland chart themselves,
as they'd prefer. For us, there's just one doubt:
that medieval England may be dimmed
by age, and all that's earlier blotted out.
X-rays might help. But surely ardent rhyme
will, as it's always claimed, outshine mere time?

By its own power the influence will rise
from sites and settlements deep underground
of those who sang about them while they stood.
Pale phosphorescent glimmers will be found
of epics chanted to pre-Roman tunes
and poems in, instead of about, runes.

Reproduced by permission of Bloodaxe Books from Fleur Adcock, *Collected Poems*.

U. A. FANTHORPE
THE FORTUNE-TELLER'S FUNERAL

The seeing has been my life. Handed down
Like silver. No use here, in Farnborough,
Where they know my proper name. But Easter-time
Sees me off on my way to Margate.
A good place to mystify. Westgate sometimes,
Or Broadstairs. All gainful addresses.

Vardo, curtains, crystal ball –
They draw the people. I'd do better in the sun,
In my big chair, holding damp gorgio hands,
Say just as true a future. But they need hocus-pocus,
The lamp, reflections, shadows, me in pearlies,
Queen Gypsy Rose Lee on the posters.

I find the future. They giggle and stare,
Helpless at belief. I muzzle what I know:
How many young women will marry twice,
How many lads die young, in sand or air.
I speak riddles: *Many will love you.*
Beware of high places, of fire and steel.
They can unravel it if they like.

My own death's different. I've planned it.
Picked my undertaker, Mister Owen,
Who did so well by Levi. The procession,
He'll see to it: six jet horses
(My Levi's pals should find a proper match),
Outrider, coachman, flowers and flowers and flowers,
Great wreath in the shape of my special chair,
Romanies walking, three hundred or so,
      Twenty thousand, I say, twenty thousand
Some in mourning, some not
      Black triangles, the gypsy Z
      They are marched through. The see-saw rattle
      Of goods trains in the night.
      Whose death is this? I will not see it.
      What country's this? A world turned upside down.
      I refuse the seeing.

The mourners go
From Willow Walk to Crofton Road,
By the Park to Farnborough Common.
Traffic jams. The Deputy Mayor
Of Margate, he'll be there to show respect.
A proper Romany funeral. Like an old queen's.
　　　The ash tree, I say, the birch tree.
Such things need to be thought about before.
　　　And the Devouring.
　　　I refuse the seeing.

My death, I know it well:
The April day in nineteen thirty-three; the weather, rainy,
And cold; the missel-thrush singing all day.
By the vardo, till I die. I am Urania,
Friend of the skies, the one who knows the future.

　　　　　I will not hear the gypsies playing in the lager.
　　　　　I will not hear it when the music stops.

'The Fortune-Teller's Funeral'. See *The Kentish Times*, 5.5.1933; Isabel Fonseca, *Bury Me Standing* (Vintage, 1996); Brian Vesey-FitzGerald, *Gypsies of Britain* (David and Charles, 1973). *The gypsy Z*: tattoo mark (for Zigeuner, meaning gypsy) used in Auschwitz-Birkenau. *Proper name*: Urania Boswell, wife of Levi. *Vardo*: Romany word for van. *Gorgio*: non-gypsy. *The Devouring*: gypsy word for the Holocaust.

ROBERT SAXTON

THE EARLIEST DAYS OF SCOUTING

On the little yellow ferry over from Sandbanks Baden-Powell taught
    twenty-two boys the word "spindrift".
Two or three of them – Lady Rodney's boys perhaps, and certainly
    Musgrave Wroughton – already knew "spendthrift".

With commendable English stealth over the dew-sodden tents
    on the heath to the south of the island crept the pale-faced dawn.
A rabbit in its sand-cave shuddered – feel the tingle in the soles
    of your bare feet? – at the cry of the African kudu horn.

Boys tumbled out of their tents to milk and biscuits
    and a strenuous half-hour of physical training.
Then came prayers and flag-hoisting – a reprise of the indomitable
    spirit their tattered Union Jack had shown at Mafeking.

After breakfast (at eight) there was a mock whale hunt race
    between the Ravens and the Curlews,
the whale being a snouted float of tree sawn, carved and smoothed
    in a craft guild comprising the two competing crews.

The Bulls and the Wolves learned how to stuff a fern mattress –
    in an *envelope* of fern, as one Harrovian Wolf boasted –
and how to mix "dampers" of dough in their pockets,
    later to be wound round sticks at the camp fire and roasted.

There was also a deer hunt, one of the boys volunteering
    to be the luckless prey – well, at least it shouldn't be boring.
The "deer" could climb trees, three tennis balls striking him denoted
    the kill, one ball striking a stalker was accounted a fatal goring.

The Poole and Bournemouth boys were taciturn –
    all that prissy public school politeness raised their hackles.
Two Etonians watched with mounting incredulous horror
    while the Purbeck monster swallowed ten raw cockles.

At seven-thirty came the compulsory rub-down, followed
    by a hunter's supper round the great heart of crackling flame.
All around them nightjars whirred and clapped – or goatsuckers,
    to use their all too graphic country name.

Then Baden-Powell sang Zulu songs, with lots of
    hard-to-remember, though repeated, vowels and consonants,
and in a kilt of cat-skins and squirrel-tails caused
    prodigious mirth performing a rooster-like Zulu dance.

Over nettle tea the camp fell silent as its famous leader
    recounted an adventure of the Matabele campaign.
"When scouting with my native boy near the Matopo Hills
    I spotted some grass that had been freshly trodden down,

"and near by on the track some footprints in the sand,
    small ones, of boys or women, moving toward the scarp
on a long march, as I learned from the sandals
    that they wore, and recent, since the edges were still sharp.

"Then the boy some distance from the track yelled out
    that he had stumbled across a leaf not native here,
from a tree that grew, oh ten to fifteen miles away.
    This leaf was damp and smelled of Xhosa beer.

"So: a party of women had come from about ten miles back
    with beer – which they tote in pots upon their heads,
the mouth of each pot stoppered with a bunch of leaves.
    (Such is the explicatory light intelligent scouting sheds.)

"They had passed at four this morning, when a strong wind blew,
    enough to carry a leaf like this yards from the track.
In about an hour they would reach the Matopos, rest awhile,
    then, balancing empty pots on their heads, thirstily amble back.

"The men would want to drink the beer while it was fresh,
    and start upon it straightaway, so if we followed the signs
to their camp we were sure to find them sleepy, guard relaxed,
    and we could reconnoitre safely – behind, as it were, their lines."

As I drifted off to sleep that night I thought of an afternoon
    when I was lying near a little stream in a rocky look-out post.
A swish of the tall yellow grass, a tinkle of trinkets –
    suddenly a naked Zulu was standing thirty feet away at most,

white tassels on arms and knees, white feathers on brow,
  offsetting rich brown skin, mock scars of the warpath,
wild cat-skins and monkey-tails adangle around his loins,
  an assegai, a dappled ox-hide shield, a yellow walking-staff

stock-still for almost a minute, like a statue cast in bronze,
  listening for anything suspicious, then with one quick bound
laying his hands upon the rocks and drinking on all fours
  like an animal, his lips making a thirsty sucking sound,

so I could see them in my mind's eye touch the water
  suck, scarcely a pause, suck pause suck, voraciously.
He drank for it seemed an age, rose and picked his weapons up,
  listened a minte then moved away, a leaf far from its tree.

ILYSE KUSNETZ
SMALL CHANGE

Curious, copper's affinity for the floor.
How one finds it curled behind doors or setees
or in parking lots, under cars.

She said: *You are my ideal*, and he replied
Your ideals have feet of clay.
She laughed and snatched a penny from his ear.

She attracts men who know a penny's value
is no more and no less than the sum
of its presidential head between its monumental tail,

A penny saved. And she wonders
what science compels her to pause every time,
to pick up, to take in, the small change.

GRAHAM MORT
DISTANCE

Gridlocked, the station broils in lassitude;
rails glint in angle-grinding sun, girls saunter
in short skirts, a porter shunts trolleys, a cat
woos pigeons with disingenuous charm.

An unshaven man, a woman in a yellow dress taste
a kiss, tentative as asking in a foreign tongue;
no train comes, but heat crumples hills beyond the
town hall roof, its copper cupola and lying face.

No train. The town is held at two o'clock, no ransom
for its golden hands, but girls still pass, so something
must be happening somewhere close. The cat cocks
its ears and stares, the porter wipes his face, the woman

sighs, the man rubs stubble, fumbles for a match.
Headlines wilt on the news stand, calamities
settle into columns, calmed until we read them,
feel something – nothing maybe – treading

two o'clock like water deeper than our legs.
You're screwing your heel into pink chewing
gum, sighing in your yellow frock. Elsewhere,
the train shimmers in its chemise of heat;

I smoke this cigarette, watch your breasts pant
under their glaze of salt. I'm through with kissing you,
I think, but can't say exactly why or what has snapped
loose from its attenuated moment. Pigeons parachute

from gutters, the town hall time is two, the train arrives.
I watch those girls watch a woman ask a man a question
which slakes his face the way dust takes rain. Your eyes
brim with slamming doors and you're asking me again,

What's wrong? What's wrong?
All this, I say, taking your arm, taking the pulse
of your body's closeness to mine, its distance
from the sun. *All this.*

CAROLYN KIZER
THE ASHES

This elderly poet, unpublished for five decades,
Said that one day in her village a young girl
Came screaming down the road:
"The Red Guards are coming! The Red Guards
Are coming!" At once the poet
Ran into her house and stuffed the manuscript
Of her poems into the stove. The only copy.
When the guards arrived they took her into the yard
For interrogation. As they spoke
The poet's mother tried to hang herself in the kitchen
That's all I know about the Red Guard.
It is enough.

The elderly poet is bitter – and why not?
She earned her Ph.D. at an Ivy League school
And returned to China in 1948. Bad timing.
She is bitter with me
Because I've chosen to translate a younger poet,
Young enough to be her child, or mine.
The truth is, her poems are pedestrian,
Uninspired. The good work died in the stove.
She knows this. She wants me to recompose them
From the ashes. She wants the noose
Around her mother's neck untied by me.
She wants – oh she wants! – to have her whole life over:

Not to leave America in 1948;
To know me when we are both young promising poets;
Her rusty English now is flawless,
My Mandarin, so long unused, is fluent.
No dictionaries needed. A perfect confidence
Flowing between us. And the Red Guard,
Except as the red sword-lilies
That invigilate the garden,
Unimagined by us both:
I who believe the Reds are agrarian reformers,
She who believes she will be an honored poet,
Her name known to everyone, safe in her fame.

HUGH MACPHERSON
A POSTCARD OF CHINTU HORSE FAIR

This postcard crackles cardboard in my hand
like wind snapping in the tether ropes:
the horses' manes stream out with the willows
caught in the morning breeze that brings
the metal scent of mountain snows
to our flat lands, where every kind of green
breathes today across the meadows
in patches of fierce-growing herbs and moss,
hiding their rage to live under a calm exterior
that fools none of their botanic competitors
extending a sly leaf into alien territory
– while the mild horses graze bemused above.

For them too there's a tense satisfaction
in this sharp wind, that makes tails lash restlessly:
they can feel it's a day to set out for somewhere,
to buy a horse, nuzzle up to its clouding breath,
tell it softly I'll be kind, the mountain air
will suit us both, and feel it under way beneath me,
anxious to get moving now as both horse and I spot a pair
of high eagles shrugging easily towards our destination.
The river shows us in single silhouette as we contemplate
the crossing. Clouds join the picture, arranging themselves
in macho pose against the wind's energy with a quiff of vapour
carefully displayed. I'm glad we've begun this journey.

Then I look up from river and postcard, gaze out
from my New York diner and take in the Manhattan street,
with across the road the balcony with its eccentric
objets trouvés arranged to entertain the world,
its whirl of children's wind stars blowing round on their tall sticks
while the rococo flamingo throws out colour in a blast
that nearly spooks the Texan palomino toy into the traffic,
his painted tan flaking on his forehead. I recognise the continuity
of this, feeling the breeze tug avidly at the wind stars
that birl and torque impatiently. It's time to scrawl some words
of greeting on the card, stick on a hasty stamp, and stride out
in Mexican boots to head for the southern pastures.

RODDY LUMSDEN
AGAINST NATURISM

I realise it's not all salad sandwiches
at pinewood picnics, endless volleyball.
I've heard the arguments that talk of shame
and how our forebears thought their bodies *dirty;*
how we've all got one. Seen one, seen 'em all.

But it's not for me, beneath my double load
of Calvinist and voyeuristic tendencies.
For me, I have to see the clothes come off:
the way a button's thumbed through cotton cloth –
a winning move in some exotic game

with no set rules but countless permutations –
or how a summer dress falls to the floor
with momentary mass and with a plash
that stirs us briefly as we ply our passion;
a hand pushed through the coldness of a zip,

three fingertips that follow down the spine
to where a clasp is neatly spun undone
amidkiss, by prime legerdemain
and who cares that it happens once in four
and never, *never* on the first undressing,

it must be better than a foreskin snagged
on gorse thorns or a cold, fat nipple jammed
in the scissor drawer, the bounty and the blessing,
the mystery of nakedness reduced
till on a par with go-go palaces

where goosebumped, grinding strippers strut their stuff
in the birthday clothes of backstreet empresses,
down on a par with the oncologist
who gropes for lumps, the night-morgue man who clips
his nails amongst the naked, bin-bagged stiffs.

So, stranger, what I want to say is this:
if you're to join me in a little sinning

(and this is my place up here on the right),
please understand I'd value some reluctance,
a cold-feet shiver, as in the beginning

when Eve discovered modesty and slipped
in and out of something comfortable.
Though there are many ways to skin a cat,
ours is human nature – things come off
so rarely. Come in. Let me take your coat.

VOYEUR

I ask her, what's sexy? *Watching*, she says.
But watching what? Four strangers making love?
No. Seeing what you're not supposed to see?

No. Thrilling yourself in a hall of mirrors?
Glimpsing the ocean? Looking over the edge
and knowing just how easy it would be? *No.*

How about watching our awkward shape hauled
into the net at last? The gup of a toad's throat
springing back into place? *No. Just watching.*

How about watching the foreshore folding
and folding its constant hunch of luck?
The lone, long walker reaching home at last?

No. Watching a bass string throb and settle
at the end of the final song? The island ferry
returning late and empty, bumping the jetty?

The long cosh of a thaw? An advancing swarm?
No. Just watching, she says and stares
as the ocean booms beyond the window.

Her tea-green eyes. Her brazen hair.
The malt-musk of Laphroaig about her mouth.
The rutting motion of the rocking chair.

THE REVIEW PAGES

The Debt to Pleasure

HARRY CLIFTON ON THOM GUNN

THOM GUNN

Boss Cupid

Faber, £7.99
ISBN 0 571 202985

Muscled and veined, not
a bad old body
for an old man.

('The Artist as an Old Man')

POETS, AS READILY as anyone else, can tend in old age to disown their own pasts. Not so Thom Gunn, whose attitude is as well encapsulated in this lyric by the Greek poet Cavafy as in anything he himself has written.

> I didn't restrain myself. I gave
> in completely and went,
> went to those pleasures that
> were half real,
> half wrought by my own mind,
> went into the brilliant night
> and drank strong wine,
> the way the champions of
> pleasure drink.

Those unregenerate champions of pleasure, aware all the time of the ephemerality of their ecstasies but generous withal, to themselves and to others, are the presiding presences in this book. Where life is the life of the body, and no real transcendence is hoped for or believed in, what is left is memory, affection, loyalty of a kind. Pleasure and the consequences of pleasure, the young body that becomes the old body, the destiny of the flesh, turn Gunn's battle-scarred veterans of homosexual love into emblems oddly reminiscent of Seamus Heaney's disco watcher ("I felt like some old pike all badged with sores / wanting to swim in touch with soft-mouthed life"). Fleshly selves, suffering their own physical dissolution with open eyes.

> Vulnerable because
> Naked because His own model.

> ...unregenerate champions of pleasure, aware all the time of the ephemerality of their ecstasies but generous withal, to themselves and to others, are the presiding presences in this book. Where life is the life of the body, and no real transcendence is hoped for or believed in, what is left is memory, affection, loyalty of a kind...

Where he and Cavafy part, however, is in the presence or absence of a context for the spasms of bodily joy. Cavafy's boys and men, when the appointed hour is over, fall away into a whole safety net of Graeco-Alexandrian politics and history, two thousand years of it, that tells them they are more than just instruments of an issueless pleasure, but part of a fabric larger than themselves. The same cannot be said of the bars and bath-houses of San Francisco, or the parks, flats and underpasses of New York where Gunn sets many of these encounters, and whose habitués walk away afterwards, it would seem, into an American void. That, perhaps, is their heroism, the attempt to elevate, out of some anonymous locker-and-steam-room joint called The Barracks, a pleasure-city of the intense instant, before the plague-rashes appear and the place burns down.

> If, furthermore,
> Our Dionysian experiment
> To build a city never dared before
> Dies without reaching to its full extent,
> At least in the endeavour we translate
> Our common ecstasy to a brief ascent
> Of the complete, grasped paradisal state
> Against the wisdom pointing us away.

('Saturday Night')

If there is any context at all for the bodies seeking bodies, it is in art rather than politics. Many of those celebrated, commemorated or simply met in passing, are fellow-poets, artists, would-be writers or male muses, instruments of Cupid. At times, the whole body-drama is projected backwards right through history into myth, most successfully perhaps in 'A Wood near Athens'.

> A wedding entertainment about love
> Was set one summer in a wood near Athens.
> In paintings by Attila Richard Lukacs,
> Cadets and skinheads, city boys, young Spartans
> Wait poised like ballet-dancers in the wings
> To join the balance of the corps in dances
> Passion has planned. They that have power, or seem
> to,
> They that have power to hurt, they are the constructs
> Of their own longing, born on the edge of sleep,
> Imperfectly understood.

That is as near as Gunn comes to providing a satisfactory context for the love-games and in some way eternising them. No real landscapes or backdrops are elaborated on, where geography might have replaced history, no city is made particular for living or dying into. In the absence of transcendence, no real tragedy is possible either, only regret. The dead, who at best leave a few memory-traces, are eulogised in a minor key.

> They are no good to me, of no value to me but
> I cannot shake them and do not want to. Their
> story, being part of mine, refuses to reach an
> end. They present me with new problems, surprise
> me, contradict me, my dear, my everpresent dead.
> ('Postscript: The Panel')

It may be objected that the gay fantasisings and reminiscences, the half-wistful eyeing up of young talent and the elderly gratitude for sexual favours received, can seem too narrow a subject-matter for someone who ought to have more than that to say about the world. Unfairly, I think, for every poet works within his or her obsessional circle, admitting only one or two central complexes of feeling, the rest belonging to the discursive realm outside. If there is variety, it is of style rather than subject. The ghosts of old masters from the free and stanzaic past are played off against each other, be they Auden, Roethke (imitating Yeats), blank-verse Shakespeare, even the slippered complacencies of

the later James Fenton. But behind it all lies Gunn's apprenticeship under Yvor Winters, himself divided between the free demotic of William Carlos Williams and the moral and stanzaic toughness of Elizabethans like Fulke Greville. The Williams-self of Gunn occupies a middle section called 'Gossip', and is pitched in a loose, democratic mode of direct address.

> J.J.
> he said, J.J.,
> that's my name.
> Talked, that time, of getting something published
> – So you write, I said!
> Why, didn't you know,
> his smile triumphant, I was
> Frank O'Hara's last lover.
> ('Famous Friends')

This is bracketed, on either side, by Campion-like lyrics that express Gunn's Elizabethan self, and seem designed to be set to lute music and sung. Whatever the mode, though, the tone is always mild, hovering somewhere between the crises of the past and something not quite wisdom or resignation, but almost.

> When I switched off my light I was dog-tired
> But for some minutes held off sleep: I heard
> The pleasant sound of voices from next door
> Through windows open to the clement darkness.
> A dinner for the couple one floor up
> Married today. I hardly had the time
> Before falling away, to relish it,
> The sociable human hum, easy and quiet
> As the first raindrops in the yard, on bushes,
> heard similarly from bed. Chatting, the sounds
> Of friendliness and feeding often broken
> By laughter. It's consoling, Mr. Love,
> That such conviviality is also
> One more obedience to your behest,
> The wedding bed held off by the wedding feast.
> ('To Cupid')

Behind that, like an aged Prospero with his business done, or an agent of Cupid, lies the later Auden. The love-game is for others now, one is a survivor, but one doesn't disclaim or forget.

You can order this book POST-FREE from the PBS at £7.99. See p.85 for details.

Love & Regeneration

by Ian Tromp

GERALD STERN

This Time: New and Selected Poems

W.W. Norton, £9.95
ISBN 0 393 31909 1

THIS TIME RECORDS "a lifetime of tearful singing" ('Orange Roses'), gathering work from seven of Gerald Stern's published volumes and adding to them fourteen new poems. Stern's voice is full of "sweetness and clarity" ('Days of 1978'), his poems sorrowful and intimate and funny.

Though "Oh there is so much shit in the universe" ('Your Animal')' Stern writes frequently with good humour and playfulness. I found especially moving several of the poems dedicated to his friends (a few for Robert Summers, and others for poets W. S. Merwin, Philip Levine, James Wright and Richard Hugo), which are particularly intimate and affectionate. Other poems, such as 'Pick and Poke' and 'Grapefruit' demonstrate a self-effacing archness, playing with language and with narrative to undermine the seriousness of their topic. And even in a poem such as 'Picking the Roses', which speaks of "collecting / all the stupidity and sorrow / of the universe in one place", there is an air of celebration and rejoicing.

Though he often begins his poems with a simple description or declaration –"I love to sit down" ('Elaine Comparone'), or "Today I'm sticking a shovel in the ground" ('Bee Balm') – he ranges out, expanding themes associatively. In 'The Dancing', for instance, personal retrospect meshes with contemporary events when the view extends beyond a young man dancing in 1945 –

> [...] my knives all flashing, my hair all streaming,
> my mother red with laughter, my father cupping
> his left hand under his armpit, doing the dance
> of old Ukraine, the sound of his skin half drum,
> half fart, the world at last a meadow

– to take in "5,000 miles away / [...] the other dancing – in Poland and Germany". So the dancing here, on "Beechwood Boulevard [...] in Pittsburgh, beautiful filthy Pittsburgh" stretches around the world toward European Jewry a year into World War II. This passage demonstrates, too, Stern's ear for the rhythms of language, playing pacing against the line to make a breathless music.

Song and music are recurring motifs in *This Time*. In 'Singing', he remarks on "how long it took to convert / death and sadness into beautiful singing"; in 'Romania, Romania', he writes: "It's only music that saves me." 'Weeping and Wailing' describes the sad music of the jew's-harp:

> My hand goes up and down like a hummingbird.
> My mouth is opening and closing. I am singing
> in harmony, I am weeping and wailing.

But the most fitting passage to quote is the closing line of 'Christmas Sticks', a poem of remarkable imaginative breadth (it is, after all, about two sticks left on the porch, "so they can talk to each other about poor Poland"). The poem ends with a phrase that articulates one thread of *This Time*, one melody of its music: the sticks are described as "singing songs about love and regeneration".

What strikes one about Stern's work is that he is so *unrestrained*: in joy and grief, these poems seem to hold nothing back; they are uninhibited in their emotionality, wholehearted and frank and energetic. And though rooted in the body ('Your Animal' describes itself as "a poem against gnosticism / [...] a poem against the hatred of the flesh") and in the everyday, Stern's poems often have a spiritual and even a mystical atmosphere. It is primarily in their empathy that one witnesses this quality: for animals, for friends, for strangers, Stern evokes a rare warmth and kindliness. In an early poem he imagines a place with "women and men of all sizes and all ages / living together without satire" ('The Unity'). In the United States, *This Time* was awarded the 1998 National Book Award for poetry, a prize sometimes said to be second in significance only to the Pulitzer. Stern is frequently compared to Whitman – Kate Daniels in the *Southern Review* described him as "a post-nuclear, multicultural Whitman for the millennium", a facile accolade, but one which communicates something of the ardour Stern provokes in his readers. What he shares with Whitman is largesse and kindness and empathy, and reading him one takes delight in the breadth of his vision, the extent of his heart.

You can order this book POST-FREE from the PBS at £9.95. See p.85 for details.

Serendipity

by Douglas Houston

TIM LIARDET

Competing With the Piano Tuner

Seren, £7.95
ISBN 1 85411 227 9

PAUL GROVES

Eros and Thanatos

Seren, £7.95
ISBN 1 85411 254 6

MIKE JENKINS

Red Landscapes

Seren, £8.95
ISBN 1 85411 244 9

JOHN POWELL WARD

Late Thoughts in March

Seren, £7.95
ISBN 1 85411 250 3

SHEENAGH PUGH

Stonelight

Seren, £7.95
ISBN 1 85411 243 0

DUNCAN BUSH

Midway

Seren, £7.95
ISBN 1 85411 226 0

DERYN REES-JONES

Signs Round a Dead Body

Seren, £6.95
ISBN 1 85411 241 4

PAUL HENRY

The Milk Thief

Seren, £6.95
ISBN 1 85411 240 6

IT'S ENCOURAGING TO begin this piece with no generalization worth making about these eight books from Seren, the principal Welsh publisher of poetry and fiction in English. Most of the work here has outgrown the debate about what "Anglo-Welsh poetry" is, or should be, that was loudly conducted within the principality, and largely ignored beyond it, in recent decades. The term has found its definitions in Anthony Conran's *The Cost of Strangeness* (1982) and *Frontiers in Anglo-Welsh Poetry* (1997), freeing poets, critics, and publishers to begin moving beyond the constraining anxieties of cultural identity.

Tim Liardet

Tim Liardet puts in a stylish performance in *Competing With the Piano Tuner*, though his characteristic inventiveness can get the better of him. 'Celsius', for example, an ambitious poem in eleven long rhyming stanzas, fails in its attempt to invest the dry summer of 1995 with the status of an epic drought. The energy with which it mixes minute observation and hyperbole is abundant but oddly internalized. As the poem goes about the business of extending itself, the reader begins to feel excluded. The same gift for sustaining an impulse pays off well, however, elsewhere. 'Mirror Angled at Sky' surprises with the rewarding poetic mileage in a broken mirror among builders' rubble. Elegy and lyric celebration interpenetrate "where nature and something else conflate", descriptive precision forming a basis for the imaginative lift-off achieved. It moves through the implications of an inconsequential remark about a mirror by Dr Johnson to a glimpsed metaphysics of cloud. Like many here, the poem is idiosyncratically well made, understated rhyme in an unusual stanza form offering a firm structural principle. The iambic drive in some of Liardet's work is apparent in 'The Scutter's Song', a poem alive with the vitality of the women it celebrates:

Oh, the great nets swarm. The bucket swills
towards our knives and our quick humour is
made slippery with those lush obscenities
that slide like the salmons' spleens, into the bins.

'The Nettled Spring', which enters with sympathetic detachment into a pregnant girl's psychosis, may be the best thing in the book. Divergent clinical and subjective realities are both encompassed by the humane lucidity of the narrating voice, which effects a brilliantly judged conclusion, charged with a shock of imminent birth. Beyond its registrations of economic hardship in Eastern Europe, 'Olga Speaking Broken English' ("I come here in America a professing dancer for the hasty payment") is the most amusing poem in a book that frequently sends out ripples of wit.

Paul Groves

Paul Groves has a talent to amuse that gives rise to some entertaining pieces and flickers across the surfaces of much of his work. Sometimes this serves to maintain an interesting detachment from the conventions of seriousness, though occasional poems seem to falter between earnestness and the gratifications of light verse. 'The Dog's Funeral' succeeds bizarrely in having it both ways, and ends on a disconcertingly deadpan note: "It was a quite disgusting day. / Dogs are evil. I'm certain of that". *Eros and Thanatos* is as good as its title, containing little if anything that has no bearing on either love or death. As themes they're present in about equal measure and co-exist in numerous poems. There's a disarming relaxation about 'Getting Down To It', an unassumingly conversational treatment of married love and the attractions of being buried together. Groves keeps the wolves of grief at a distance. 'A Particular Woman' gains stature as an elegy for his mother from its unflappable tone. Resolute avoidance of emotional gesture is particularly effective in 'Endgame', which takes us through the last hours of an American prisoner condemned to death. Rhyme qualifies the cold functionality of the concise sentences, while the carrying over of full rhymes between expertly crafted stanzas serves to mute the poem's music. It works on pure description, behind which is sensed all the pressure of terrible understatement. 'The Empty Step' is another highly effective poem that benefits from the leavening of rhyme and the detachment conferred by strict form. It deftly charts the descent into heroin addiction of a subject who remains unidentified, though domestic allusions make powerful suggestions. The last stanza effects irrevocable closure, in any sense of the word:

> Smack closed the door,
> brought down the ceiling,
> opened the floor.

John Powell Ward

John Powell Ward's work could benefit from some-thing of the wit and detachment that sharpen the verse of Liardet and Groves. There's a sincerity and conscientiousness about *Late Thoughts in March* which issues in undeviatingly scrupulous addresses to places and occasions – the airport, the concert, the harvest, current events. Elsewhere, his writing arrives from a point where rational discourse and the liberating resources of the imagination merge. In the eight sections of 'She Wrote to Me' the vivid disjunctions of dreaming, with which Ward deals well in other poems, are held in balance by the openness and vitality of tone and imagery. The poem marshals its domestic and quotidian motifs against compliance with the chaos that disorders its rational surfaces. Strange things result:

> After the night, when the new pen was delivered,
> I made a box for paints, and kept the song
> In a plastic wrapper, as the gardening manuals
> Decreed.

'Hallucination' combines an estranging glimpse of "The daughter I never had" with the bare factuality conveyed by shrewd use of a Larkinesque note of regret:

> I had two brothers and their dad
> Was just an only, like his wife.
> A kind of thin, one-gendered life.

The accomplishment in such lines makes it very odd that Ward repeatedly commits deforming inversions elsewhere. "Redeemed are for me the underpinning thought / And first colour" concludes the unmanageable first stanza of 'A Third Place', while lines on the Wye contain the embarrassing "Fertile waits its valley" and "New moments to crave".

Mike Jenkins

Mike Jenkins's *Red Landscapes* is a similarly uneven collection. Impressively original material is thrown into contrast against the sociological continuum of his prevailing concerns and approaches. Jenkins displays the same constraining loyalty to locality and community that marks the work of Idris Davies (1905 – 1953). Both are unmistakeably voices for the inarticulate and imaginatively impoverished mining valleys of South Wales and can allow the obligation to be plainly heard and understood to get the better of poetry. Jenkins succeeds most forcefully in appealing to social justice when he depicts the violence and squalor of lives brutalised by economics, a world of

> women about to give birth
> to washing-machines, women whose blue-mould
> bruises are painted over with make-up.

'Once a Musical Nation' manages to stay in touch with humour as it registers the frightening ignorance and intolerance of a culture shrunk to TV. A totalitarianism of the absent imagination prevails, and newcomers suspected of dissent are under surveillance:

> Why carn they ave a satellite saucer
> Like ev'ryone else? There's effin 'n' blindin,
> It's all in my diary, written down.

South Wales dialect is used recurrently in this generous "new and selected" from Jenkins. He's at his best in this effective vein in some of the school poems, each of which is underwritten by his decades as a teacher. 'Mouthy' is a rare success, a poem that seems equal in its appeal to both children and adults. Like 'Once a Musical Nation', it's an unsettling testimony to the late twentieth-century decay of anything much resembling a culture:

> Sborin, sir!
> We're always doin racism.
> It's that or death, sir.
> Yew're morbid, yew are,
> Or gotta thing about the blacks.

The "New Poems" section contains several prose-poems, most notably 'His Last Demonstration'. This is a powerfully haunting piece, blending images of clinical pathology and artistic creation to suggest a dream-elegy for its unnamed subject. It's a high point in a collection that achieves the success of at least being invariably readable.

Sheenagh Pugh

Sheenagh Pugh is likewise reader-friendly. Her work's accessibility is a feature of the clarity and inevitability with which she can pursue intuitions into territories of luminous significance. An imaginative affinity with the Euclidean emptinesses of the polar regions in *Stonelight* runs through 'The Arctic Chart' sequence and has its finest product in the Forward Prize-winning 'Envying Owen

Beattie'. The poem flows forward on a surge of fascination and reverence as Beattie and his men thaw out a body preserved in ice since the early nineteenth-century. The risky eroticism of the closing images is firmly anchored to the more factual "rush / that reckless trust sends / through parents and lovers" that accompanies the earlier lifting of the body. Northerly latitudes provide a sanctuary for affirmation in the Shetland poems, paeans to unspoiled nature and glad immediacy of experience in "air too ruthlessly pure to screen out the sun" ('Postcard'). 'Far Places' exemplifies the sympathetic identification with other lives on which a number of Pugh's poems are based. The ageing walker's realization that "every, distant, high, uncommon place / is getting further" is part of the apparatus of elegiac understatement through which the poem registers universal transience and loss. Elsewhere, her judgement occasionally yields to a sententious impulse to extend a conclusion already clearly inscribed in a poem. 'Bryn Asaph' carries on beyond the possibility of ending very well on the *"Before this, nothing was"* that closes the penultimate stanza. Overall, though, *Stonelight* makes clear Pugh's gift for combining a firm grounding in common experience with an imaginative idealism that illuminates the factual surfaces of her work.

Duncan Bush

Duncan Bush gets off to a good start in *Midway* with 'Uncle Charlie', which initially assumes the familiar form of the "my incorrigible elderly relative" poem. It's a good example of the genre, but a generous follow-through raises it to a higher order. After alluding to Charlie's war, it confronts the aftermath of heroism and victory as they are betrayed into the shabby routine of subsequent decades:

> it's 1958 or '62,
>
> and you're looking from a window
> at your old khaki drill trousers
> pegged out drying on the line for work,
> as penniless as you are, both pockets out...

A similar change of gear occurs in 'Old Prosser', which accumulates detailed recollections of its subject up to the point at which he is left staring from a window as death approaches. Suddenly, a visionary lyricism floods the poem, bearing its last five stanzas through one continuous sentence, benignly diffusing the old man in a transforming tableau of memory. The unbroken fluency of Bush's writing at this point makes extracting for quotation implausible, but it's a technical and imaginative performance worthy of anyone writing today. 'And Suddenly It's Evening' offers another demonstration of a single sentence epiphanically expanding through a long succession of supple cadences. The immediate post-war past looms large in *Midway*, a title bearing chiefly on Bush's recognition that middle-age is upon him. Childhood and the 1950s are recurrently invoked. The book includes a substantial essay entitled 'Lash LaRue and the River of Adventure', which interweaves autobiography and a provocative socio-cultural critique of the era. There are some hard-hitting poems in this collection. Several varieties of fool are not suffered gladly in, for example, 'Cousin Colin', 'Poetess', and 'Learning to Write: a Tutorial'. A failure to pull punches ultimately affirms the honesty Bush seems to suggest is the least human beings deserve. This is Bush at his best to date. A broadened command of technical possibilities enhances his forms and rhythms, while heightened narrative instincts give sharp focus to his work's concern with society and the individual.

Deryn Rees-Jones

Like Bush, Deryn Rees-Jones can use extended syntax to sustain undercurrents of rhythm as her accumulating clauses build into exploratory, sometimes incantatory, sentences. 'What It's Like To Be Alive' is a fine example. It progresses for seventeen lines through the persuasive ebb and flow of successive "and I remember" constructions, then suddenly steps back to impose perspective in the two clipped, one-line sentences at the end. There's a refreshing abundance of energy in *Signs Round a Dead Body*. Vividly sensory, it teems with sharp images and inventive approaches to the emotional, physical, and imaginative interactions making up love relationships. There's an opulent awareness, subjective and objective, of the body, which is treated with a combination of anatomical candour and exotic figurings that constantly imply celebration of the senses:

> the fishermen, the midnight seas,
> had been tattooed like hieroglyphs
> in blues and golds

> deep into her skin. It was his hands, I think,

she could imagine best,
travelling across her.

('Making Out')

The nine parts of 'Songs of Despair' retain a celebratory vitality, but cast love in bleak world of troubled retrospection. Snow and the sea are repeatedly invoked to provide a sense of blank, undifferentiated expanses evocative of emotional exhaustion and numbness. It's highly atmospheric and occasionally disturbing in its violent honesty. At the end there's a sudden connection with the symbolic energies of Coleridge's albatross that effects closure with considerable economy and force:

> see
>
> Now the scar on my breast
> A starry bullet
>
> Where, as I leapt and soared,
> With foam in my hair on that tiny raft,
>
> Thoughtlessly as a smile,
> An illegible glance,
>
> You looked up, crowing, shot me.

Paul Henry

Paul Henry, too, puts the sea to impressive use in much of *The Milk Thief*. There's a spaciousness and well-lit clarity about his best work that allows an informal directness to co-exist with occasionally cryptic feats of compression. In 'Aber', a doomed fisherman sails out across surfaces where the mythological and the factual blend seamlessly. No simile or metaphorical construction frames the imagery when the mackerel he catches become envelopes yielding letters as their bellies are slit. The poem's fluid imaginative development on the voyage out "across no man's time" has already created conditions in which such magic realism can just happen. The third of the five movements making up this remarkable poem gives the texts of a bundle of such letters addressed to figures from classical myth. For over twenty five lines the poem makes delightful music by sustaining two rhyme-sounds, producing lyrics in which formal refinement, simplicity, and gentle wit luminously combine:

> *I think about you less each day.*

The stars and the moon drift away.
The harbour's chimed jewellery
Trickles back into the sea.
I think about you less each day...

'The Hourglass' is similarly confident and convincing in its combinations of continuity and disjunction. It's an eight-part collage in which incidents and atmospheres from childhood float in imaginative suspension, a tone of amused affection constantly overriding elegiac and nostalgic possibilities. An incisive glint of affectionately ironic humour sharpens many of Henry's poems, including more conventionally anecdotal successes like 'The Last Throws of Summer', on the British Boomerang Champion, and 'Newport East', which features the *Untergang* of Arthur Scargill:

The Town's coral gathers about them –
The sun and Arthur Scargill,
Going down together,
One gracefully, one burning still.

Henry is a refreshingly original poet, and technically gifted in the making of forms whose tensile minimalism can support profound emotional implications. His work, and much else in the books considered above, gives reason for thinking that Welsh poetry in English has no reasons for prolonging its habitual crisis of confidence.

You can order these books POST-FREE from the PBS. See p.85 for details.

Dedicated To You But You Weren't Listening

by David Kennedy

HUGO WILLIAMS

Billy's Rain

Faber, £7.99
ISBN 0 571 20086 9

WHAT SHALL WE say in our reviews of Hugo Williams? That he's writing in much the same way as he was thirty years ago, an easygoing confessional poetry where important last lines hang over the reader's head like an axe hidden in a crystal chandelier? That he's fast approaching sixty but still writes a young man's poetry of affairs and cafes and hotel rooms, a kind of poetry as *Hello* magazine which shows us a lifestyle that looks like fun but which we probably wouldn't want? Williams is, after all, one of those who, in the convention of biographical notes, "divides his time" between apparently desirable locations. Biographical notes are, of course, attractive fictions and *Billy's Rain* recounts a love affair in fifty-one poems that often nod at the fictive and the self-reflexive. In the title poem the poet remembers learning on a film set that "God's rain [...]/[...] doesn't show up on film./ We need Billy's rain for this one". The poem concludes:

When I find myself soaked to the skin, tired,
or merely bored with God's rain,
the phrase comes back to me.
I'd say it now if I thought you were listening

The poem is indicative of a collection and a wider practice where art and a single self fix experience and sell it back to the reader in easily consumable portions. The important last lines I referred to make a kind of double contract with the reader. They point him or her towards a shock of recognition that "yes, life is like that"; and their irony flatters him or her that they are clever enough to share in a sophisticated insight. The irony perhaps has a further function in that it guards against both experience and conclusion being thought banal or unremarkable. The irony and the expectation of it once the first poem has been read become a kind of sexy packaging, a kind of poetic marketing strategy. And all this is perfectly pleasant and often quite amusing. Poetry which might, in the words of one poem here, be "self-pitying nonsense" is kept under control by an attractive subtext of mirrors and doubles. Several poems show us Williams watching Williams being Williams as in 'My Chances' which ends with the poet,

checking my smile
in the mirror in the hall
against my chances of being liked.

However, the fictive elements are outweighed by some very real problems. First, I think that this type of writing requires the reader to be altogether too passive in a period when even the best mainstream poetry in English from Deryn Rees-Jones to Jo Shapcott encourages the reader to participate in making the meaning. Second, in charting the course of a love affair in a style that continually asks us to admire the elegant poses of its own casualness, Williams is coming rather late to a particular party. 'Bar Italia' – one of the best poems here – in which the loved one's absence becomes paradoxically a powerful presence sent me back to Stephen Romer's first collection, *Idols*, which does this with much more depth and rhythmic invention.

Williams on Williams has always had limited appeal for me which was why *Writing Home*, about Williams's father, was such a revelation because, as Neil Corcoran points out, its 'self-revealing discriminations make contact with a whole complex of significant emotion and consciousness". *Billy's Rain*, for me, lacks similar contact complex.

Finally, *Billy's Rain* could have been written – bar a few local details – at any time during the past thirty years or so. This is partly because the book to some extent updates the earlier collection *Love-Life*. Now, it is possible to construct an argument which reads that in terms of continuity and the portrayal of universals. However, the possibility of a way of life and a mode of describing experience which we can all recognise has come to seem increasingly unlikely. Again, some of the most exciting mainstream poetry of recent years – Carson, say, or Herbert – insists that we embrace variety.

In this context, it is as if *Billy's Rain* is addressed to an imagined community where most readers will, in fact, struggle to recognise themselves. And this suggests that, if as the American critic Jerome McGann has argued, poetry is primarily humanity's way of dealing with loss and transformation, then *Billy's Rain* perhaps laments more than a lost love affair, perhaps laments more than it knows. It is as if Williams's comforting fictions insist, albeit forlornly, that more than personal realities can be fixed.

You can order this book POST-FREE from the PBS at £7.99. See p.85 for details.

ELEANOR COOKE
TALKING DIRTY

I knew some day we'd meet,
and when we met,
we'd speak a discrete language of our own.
We wouldn't have to learn it, make it up:
not like
those secret-society things kids do,
adding a consonant to every word,
talking backwards.

This would be like
when God says to Mohammed, "Write", and
Mohammed says "What's *write?*" and God says,
"Just do it": or
when pilgrims break into poetry, song
with that gone-out look on their faces,
and nobody knows what the fuck they're saying.
Like that.
Beautiful.
It hasn't happened yet.

The Lesson of Life

IAN SANSOM ON TOM PAULIN

TOM PAULIN

The Wind Dog

Faber, £7.99

ISBN 0 571 201687

SOMEONE SHOULD – MAYBE someone is – composing a *Collected Wit and Wisdom*, a *Table-Talk*, a *Head-Staggers* of Paulin. On Craig Raine – "an impossibly reactionary, ignorant and snobbish megalomaniac". "Paisleyism is curiously like reggae music". "To read Ricks on the hyphen is to taste that abject world of trivializing critical duncery which filled Pope with such savage despair". "Tennyson is in brilliant command of a dead language". His fulminations, full of bullying hyperbole, are about as illuminating and as close to bonkers as any sane man's can be.

Paulin is now well loved and well known for his appearances on a late-night television arts-review programme, appropriately named *Late Review*, on which he plays the wild-eyed Irishman, constantly leaning his head on his hands as if his brain were too heavy, determinedly pretending not to know about the existence of popular culture (such as late-night television arts-review programmes like *Late Review*). Cute academic stutter notwithstanding, his is a menacing presence, not unlike Robert Mitchum's Preacher in Charles Laughton's *The Night of the Hunter* (based on the novel by David Grubb), a tattoo on the one hand reading LOVE, and on the other HATE: "These letters spell out the Lesson of Life, boy!" If you look very closely at the base of the cranium, Paulin also bears a raised mark similar to a branding iron scar: POET©NORTHERN IRELAND.

The Wind Dog is Paulin's sixth book of verse. He started out as a rather watery-eyed and whimsical lyricist, but back in 1987 he published a book, *Fivemiletown*, his fourth, in which re-invented himself as a witty, raging ex-pat Symbolist. *Fivemiletown* was an important book, a work of daring and brilliance, full of boney, cracking and piercing little poems. Unfortunately – and who knows how much this has to do with all his mugging on the telly? – he seems to have spent much of his time since making himself over into a pasticheur of his own inimitable style.

Or as he might himself call it, as in the title of his new poem in defence of "what's clumsy or naïf", 'Stile':

because most critics they're
                                rented
by what's clumsy or naïf
it must never happen
that something other than
                                platonic form
or hammered gold or pure
                                gold leaf
– that gold to airy thinness
                                bate
should touch us or should
                                warm
the playful serious wondering
                                great
mischeevious child in most of us

The self-characterization here is accurate, but whereas the "mischeevious" child of *Fivemiletown* hit upon a ringing minor chord, he now seems to be flailing about, beating on drums, and flutes, and harps, trombones, euphoniums, and anything else he can get his hands on. The result: cacophony.

Ever since *Fivemiletown* – throughout *Walking a Line* (1994) – Paulin has been attempting through wordplay to convey both the weight and lift of language, the concentration, the freedom, the coming together and apart of words and meanings.

The ear, he now goes as far as to claim in *The Wind Dog*, "is the only true reader", a wonderful, typical enthusiastic overstatement which may explain why he sometimes sounds more like Doctor Seuss than James Joyce, a hairy wocket in his pocket rather than Joyce's memorable baby tuckoo: for every fulsome "bulgy bulgy river", and "chishclash" of bangles there's a thin clash of pointless repetition or a screeching analogy or equivocation, "from poplar to populace is only a short step", "the whole caper or caber". The new book's low point comes in a poem in which Paulin jokes about his surname, and which ends with the cracker, "maybe one day I'll find out / if it's Huguenot or Hugue*not*?"

Paulin's constant drilling at language throughout *The Wind Dog* can be exhilarating, but is sometimes disastrous. It's fine if he sticks to the phrase – "skreeky styrofoam", "tattery shadows" and "perpetual scringe" – but when he tries pushing deeper and further, the poems crumble and collapse. In the poem 'Drumcree Three', for example, the narrator describes how "On the day of Drumcree" he started "hackling the vine" in his back garden:

> as I got stuck into the vine
> I could hear on the news
> – on the radio news
> how the police were hacking a path
> through the Garvaghey residents
> so that a line
> of Orangemen in hundreds
> could walk – that is march –
> down to the church

Imagine for a moment you were teaching a course in creative writing and your earnest student were to offer this up to you, how on earth would you begin to explain to them exactly what was wrong with it? Tom, you might ask, tentatively, do you think a play on words is really appropriate here? Doesn't the harking from "hackling" to "hacking" and the linking of "vine" to "line" suggest some kind of equivalence between your pottering in the garden and events in Drumcree? And can this possibly be what you mean to say, or do you mean it only because you say it? *Och, away with ye*, might come the reply. *Shall I tell you the tale of Right-Hand-Left-Hand – the tale of Good and Evil?*

But let's stay in Northern Ireland for a moment. (Paulin himself returns for the occasional reading – which he now commemorates in a poem in *The Wind Dog*, beginning with the wilting lines, "We're catching the shuttle Hugo Williams and me / to give a poetry reading in Belfast"). The title of the new book derives from a phrase which occurs in a scrap of dialogue in the long title poem 'The Wind Dog': "– what's a wind dog captain? / – ack a wee broken bitta rainbow". *The Wind Dog*'s gusty blurb picks up on this and states categorically that "In the north of Ireland, a 'wind dog' is a fragment of rainbow". In years to come students will doubtless be parrotting this portentous "fact" in their essays, so it may be worth noting that I have been able to find no-one from "the north of Ireland" who has ever even heard the expression.

Which is what Paulin does in his preachy poem 'The Quinn Brothers'. The Quinn Brothers – Richard (10), Mark (9) and Jason (7) – were killed in a fire-bomb attack on their home in Ballymoney on the twelfth of July 1998. (The other famous Irish performing poet, Paul Durcan, happens also to have written a poem about the death of the three boys, published in his most recent collection, *Greetings to our friends in Brazil*. One might like to compare and contrast the two poems – doubtless on campuses across the country people already are – or one might prefer simply to knock their heads together.)

After the opening obligatory outlandish metaphor comparing the coffins to "those little white boxes / each with a moist square / of wedding-cake / but bigger much bigger" – a metaphor surely plucked from a notebook, and whose effect in context is to suggest the boy's deaths were some of kind of ritual gift, or, worse, a celebration – Paulin's poem wanders deep into the apocalyptic and symbolic, where the eye of a "droll / distrustful green pig" who "might be death" looks back at the council house's "orange flames", and the "feathery fabulous powerless tree". This is Paulin the Preacher – the over-reacher – no more and no less, and no other: *Now he thrust his fingers together, left hand and right hand, and now they wrung and twisted one another until the knuckles crackled horribly... And at the last word he brought both hands down with a crash to the table top*. It is a terrible sight to behold.

You can order this book POST-FREE from the PBS at £7.99. See p.85 for details.

The Return of Freddie the Dolphin

by John Goodby

IAN DUHIG

Nominies

Bloodaxe, £6.95

ISBN 1 845224 45 7

IAN DUHIG'S WORK clearly poses a problem for a certain kind of English reviewer. Tim Kendall's dismissive account (in *Poetry Review*) of his last collection, *The Mersey Goldfish*, found evidence of the "hopeless enterprise of trying to out-Muldoon Muldoon", a falling off in Duhig's talent for "redemptive humour", and much "obscurity" and "puerile" over-allusiveness. The first claim rested on a patronising inability to read poets of Irish provenance unless through a (very anglicised) version of Muldoon, while the second pointed to a dubiously religious notion of what of humour ought to do. "Obscurity" and the rest were more damaging charges; some of Duhig's poems undoubtedly made few concessions to the reader unused to his range of reference (albeit most problems could be cleared up by resort to *Brewer's*). Kendall's attack smacked suspiciously of fogeyish put-down; a poet who had been treated as a colourful but marginal figure was now demanding more attention than he could possibly be worth. Arguably, Duhig's perceived impropriety and bad taste, his yoking of cultural hybrids and the wayward energies of the Grotesque, upset notions of the poetically proper, making it difficult to fit him into the pigeonholes "London-Irish origins" and "Catholic-background". Whatever, the affront registered showed that what was at stake was not only stylistic – Duhig's dazzling miscegenation of high and low registers, coarseness and delicacy – but concerned larger issues. If, for Duhig, history was a black joke perpetrated on the dispossessed, he was never likely to see eye to eye with a Home Counties faith in gradualism and compromise.

More focussed than *The Bradford Count*, more accessible than *The Mersey Goldfish*, Nominies nevertheless advances the earlier interest in fruit-fully hybrid identities and the darker corners of history, and brings them to bear on the present to comic and frequently shocking effect. Duhig augments his blends of Irish, British and other (often wildly disparate) cultures, with northern Dark Ages, Scandinavian-Celtic elements, drawn from a time when identities such as "English", "British" or "Irish" were fluid or non-existent, adding Beccán, Saint Cuthbert and Snorri Sturluson to the wild and wonderful cast of his earlier work. This is Basil Bunting and Ken Smith territory – a chilly, ghost-ridden region of hard-bitten survivors – but made fresh by Duhig's unrooted vision, and his ransacking of oral tradition and folklore in the form of children's rhymes, saws, riddles, ballads, shanties and songs. The individual and anonymous voice blend seamlessly; 'Shanty' bears Duhig's sardonic hallmark and at the same time manages to be a wholly credible piece of orature: "Seven fly, / salmon feast. / Seven salmon; / seal feast. / Seven seal; / shark feast. / Seven shark; / whale feast. / Seven whale; / Norse feast. / Seven / Norse; / fly feast".

Elsewhere, contemporary usages are folded into the period mix with the usual eclectic gusto; the cairn of tributes to 'Fenris, wolf to Loki' includes a strawberry condom / ribbed for extra sensitivity". In addition, Duhig ranges to Navajo as a WWII code, Greek myth and an invented troubadour form, the godknowswhat, as well as subjects drawn from his own vigorous urban oral culture with its rituals of combative badinage and self-mocking identity assertion.

However, *Nominies* has broader ambitions than extending Duhig's range of forms and subjects. If his Dark Ages charts the intermingling childhoods of the several British and Irish cultures, this collection has much to do with children and their relationship to the adult world in the centuries since, and in particular with their oral culture, parallel to, ignored by, but resistant to that of adults. "Nominies" is a Yorkshire word for childrens' chants, and the title poem, a longish ballad, offers a structure for the collection as a whole. Its epigraph – to children, the days of the year change at midday rather than midnight – sets an oppositional pattern by which children's lore undermines the wisdom of grownups (the reason children's days change at mid-day is because that is when their rituals expire – April Fool's Day being only the best-known example.) *Nominies* begins at Christmas, at noon, and offers itself to its (adult) narrator as a verbal contraption like a "music-box", with a series of "turns". But the box spins out of his control as the ghost of a boy inhabiting it pursues an eye-for-an-eye revenge narrative which marks the hours of the day as it proceeds. The starting point is a children's rhyme indicting Walter Calverley for infanticide (the incident is the subject of *A Yorkshire Tragedy*, attributed to Middleton), while the "turns" in the first half of the poem call up other victims, past and present, from a boy sold by his father as a deckhand to children burnt to death in bed-and-breakfast accommodation.

If *Nominies* is structured by reference to the hours, the water and fire associated with these voices are intended to make us think of the traditional four elements. A colour structure can be discerned too; red, but also yellow, black and white indicating different times of day and- night. Thus, at six — between dusk and dawn — the poem offers its stylised yet powerful account of a racist murder, as white eclipses black. This negation marks the narrative's mid-point; following this it shifts from realistic to fantastic registers, the adult narrator, now "John Rhymer" of folklore, pitted against the figure of the Red King, or Death. No knowledge of the folklore sources of these characters is necessary to follow the twists and turns of the poem; it's clear enough that, although fancying himself victorious in this combat, the narrator kills himself in the process and by another reversal, becomes the ghost trapped inside the "music box" of the poem. Moreover, the story reveals a structure of co-ordinates and oppositions — freedom/slavery, child/adult, death/birth — its official and anti-authoritarian cycles made clear without any blunting of the impact of individual parts.

This movement is followed by *Nominies* itself, as it moves through its various times, places and thematic concerns. But Duhig's eye on a structure does not detract from the effectiveness of the component parts, as 'Straw School' movingly demonstrates:

Her parents love her huge brown eyes and how hard
she works at school,
a school which cannot teach the pupils who have
forgotten straw...

She can plait Ivanhoe, Stanbridge, Carrick bend,
narrow twist,
Egginton twist, barley, double-barley, birdseye and
whipcord.

Lists are old-fashioned poems but I catalogue the
accomplishments
of Jenny Ibbens; dead by five a century ago who still
keeps dying.

Individually effective, a piece like 'Straw School' also reflects back, paradigmatically, on the variously woven and self-critiqueing strands of the book. While several poems are based on Duhig's own childhood, for example, many stem from his experience as a father, the two states blurring and qualifying each other. *Nominies* asks how hard it is to be a parent, as well as exploring the powerlessness of children. Thus the poet is, inevitably, supplanted by his son: "You're the river of the water of life: / my legs are dead", as he tells him. But elsewhere he inverts this model. Hence, the case of a father maintaining dominion after death in 'Aeronwy's Story', which evokes the (childlike) Dylan Thomas through the memories of his daughter. The American "culture of [Thomas's] death under glass" is bizarrely echoed by her wartime story about "being abandoned in her crib / in a glasshouse, watching the waves of Heinkels / he'd shown-defiance to by making for the pub". Sons oust fathers, fathers abandon daughters yet stay on to haunt them; such complications are common, and speak of the darker displacements informing *Nominies*; even if it is usually the child who is turned out of home by adults.

Appropriately, one of the book's structural puns may be that to "turn out" something, such as a poem, is to create; but that to do the same thing to a person is make them homeless. Here Duhig's experience as a sheltered housing worker is the starting-point for a series of songs which note possible musical settings ("To the air of ..."), again emphasizing poetry's link with speech and oral culture. Far from a detour into the impenetrably archaic, Duhig's interest in the past, in orature and children's lore, proves essential to his exploration of homelessness and hopelessness. In a Britain where a hundred thousand children run away from home each year, this can hardly be "obscure", of course; but the more important point is that it is precisely the depth and range of his reference which enable Duhig to avoid the pitfalls of emptily radical political gestures.

Paradoxes and ironies inform *Nominies*, then, but of kinds both more crude and more subtle than those which have dominated much recent poetry. Recognizing that these are by no means off the radar screens of most potential readers, *Nominies* is an attempt to extend the range of what is defined as accessible poetly, entertaining us while refusing condescension and mere streetwise knowingness. The success of the attempt can be gauged in the craft of the book's structure, which reveals fresh interweavings and insights at each re-reading. But it is also apparent in the way individual poems can so suddenly and memorably lay bare Duhig's general concerns. The last word here – given Duhig's previously expressed admiration for the species – might best be left with the subject of the ballad – 'Who Killed Freddie the Dolphin?' (Freddie, a note informs us, once "delighted the thousands of people who came to see him disport in Amble Harbour with amazing penile feats and healings of the sick", before being shot by a fisherman.) Reworking 'Who Killed Cock Robin?', it characteristically elaborates on "cock" to virtuosic comic effect, but just as typically makes a point about the environment and the short shrift given to the powerless and too-trusting. Gleefully anticipating Freddie's apocalyptic return and revenge, it's tempting to see in him an image of Duhig himself, deflating male pride (the killer is a "Cod Mars" who kills "fearing-Venus") and weirdly yet effectively feminising a "wand [not] crude / but somehow numinous". The piece ends on a promise of the return of "God's second Flood", when both dolphin and poet will surely come into their own

> on Northeastern green fields
> that freemasons golf in
> will ride the red tide
> and Freddie the Dolphin
>
> and when Freddie comes,
> and he will, as and when,
> like Jesus before him
> he'll be fishing for men.

Against that millennial revenge (threatened only partly in jest, it may be), trigger-happy fishermen and fishermen-reviewers should perhaps now start to prepare.

You can order this book POST-FREE from the PBS at £6.95. See p.85 for details.

Sculpting Silence

by Dennis O'Driscoll

GUILLEVIC

Carnac

Translated by John Montague
Bloodaxe, £8.95
ISBN 1 85224 393 7

Living in Poetry:
Interviews with Guillevic

Translated by Maureen Smith
Dedalus, £7.95
ISBN 1 901233 40 5

GUILLEVIC. LIKE SAPPHO or Virgil or Anon. Not Eugène, because that was what his hated mother called him; and not, as he himself jokingly suggested (by adding Carnac, his birthplace in Brittany, to a cluster of his given names), Alphonse Marie Guillevic de Carnac. His chosen name conveys something of the pithiness of his writings and *Carnac* (he favoured one-word names for his books also) wastes no words. First published in France in 1961, when its author was fifty-four, it consists of a book-length series of very short poems which ("referring to Max Planck's theory") Guillevic called "quanta": "Isn't a poem a form of energy?"

Despite his Breton birth and family background, Guillevic was never permitted to use its language during childhood: "In the state school, we were not allowed to speak Breton (or to spit on the floor)". His large output of poetry, beginning with *Terraqué* (1942), was written exclusively in French: "my mother tongue is not that of my mother". Any tenderness he may have felt for his mother tongue was certainly not matched by affection for his tongue-lashing mother, towards whom he felt a bitterness that had lost none of its sting when, at the age of seventy, he gave the interviews (rendered into convincingly conversational English by Maureen Smith) which fill the 170 fascinating pages of *Living in Poetry*. The son of a gendarme who treated him with indifference, he recalls his mother as a tyrannical, bigoted woman with "cold blue eyes" and an "ever-suspicious pointed nose" who predicted that her son "would be good for nothing, that I would die on the scaffold, that no woman would ever want me". Guillevic survived his loveless childhood in mildewed police barracks and confounded his mother's pessimistic prognosis by dying an 89-year-old, twice-married, internationally-admired poet. He worked as a civil servant and was especially busy immediately after the war when (a Party member) he served as assistant head of Cabinet for the Communist Minister of Reconstruction: "I had little time to sleep, and none for reading and writing". Any *temps perdu* was extravagantly recouped, however, when – mistrusted on political grounds by later administrations and denied meaningful tasks – he could "read the complete works of Proust in the office, and I read them slowly, page by page".

Guillevic resembles Yves Bonnefoy, as Stephen Romer's introduction to *Carnac* suggests, in being a "mystic without a God". If Communism was his surrogate God, it was one that failed only partially for him and he remained a Party member until 1980. Having, in "about 1950", penned the inevitable cant in honour of Stalin, he at least had the grace to recant when he was interviewed by Lucie Albertini and Alain Vircondelet for *Living in Poetry*: "Of course I would no longer write that", he concedes of 'To Stalin', "As a poem, it's not too bad, but it isn't true". Yves Bonnefoy recently described poetry as a "cure for ideology"; the extent of Guillevic's cure may be gauged from the disclosure to his interviewers that "I have come to the conclusion that I should mistrust myself in everything concerning politics, and that in any case I was a poet rather than a man of action".

Carnac was recognised by Guillevic himself as part of a wider recovery process – which included a recovery of his Breton inheritance: "*Carnac* was a great joy for me, a deliverance. I found myself completely, I found my country again, the land, the sea..." Portions of the poem were translated into English by Teo Savory for Penguin's *Selected Poems* (1974); an excellent rendering of the full text, by Robert Chandler, appeared in *Modern Poetry in Translation* in 1995. The Bloodaxe edition contains not only the entire poem, translated with admirable clarity and economy by John Montague, but the French text as well. While *Carnac* offers sea views in almost every section, other preoccupations also surface. These (as Stephen Romer points out)

include memories of a young love lost to meningitis, reflections on the awe-inspiring megalithic monuments of Carnac and "quanta" in which "the appeal to the feminine, in particular to the maternal" is all too understandable in the light of the poet's harsh childhood experiences.

If Wallace Stevens had written 'One Hundred and Fifty Ways of Looking at a Sea', the result might have resembled *Carnac*. Alternatively, *Carnac* could be seen as a poetical equivalent of Monet's "series" paintings or a collection of riddles (to which the answer is sometimes *la mère* and more often *la mer*). The individual sections seem as spontaneous as envelope jottings; yet they are capable of epigrammatic coherence. It is as if the poet had engaged in a process of trial and error, as if each poem were a draft that might ultimately lead to the one true poem, the one definitive revelation:

> Yes, I have seen you, wild, out of control,
> Before shouldering the assaults of the wind.
>
> I have seen you flouted, seeking your revenge
> And wreaking it on others than the wind.
>
> But I speak of you when you are only yourself,
> Without power except to absorb.

Carnac itself generates tremendous cumulative power, even if there are dull stretches when the poet's brainstorming displays too much brain and not enough storm. The exhilaration for the reader lies in the lightning-flash transitions from section to section, in the poem's inventiveness and resourcefulness, in its capacity to constantly alter course and change perspective as it tries to narrow the gulf between obsessive poet and inscrutable sea. *Carnac* frequently registers the limitations of language, like a sea pounding against barriers of rock; Stephen Romer identifies the "non-coincidence of sign with signified" as a fundamental dynamic of the poem. A poet of silences, Guillevic's pages abound in white space; and if Mallarmé (an essay about whom prompted the first stirrings of *Carnac*) could assert that poems are made not with ideas but with words, Guillevic implies *au contraire* that they are made not with words but with silences. *Carnac* is a modern megalith, "a sculpture of silence".

You can order these books POST-FREE from the PBS. See p.85 for details.

MATTHEW FRANCIS
WHAT THE CUTTLEFISH DO

Who's the girl you saw on the beach?
Is she the girl for you?
The backs of her knees are marked with an H,
her breasts are a W.

You've taken her to a hot, bright dance,
to the cold cliffs in the rain.
You've laid your arm on her shoulders
and taken it off again.

You talked over coffee and biscuits,
you talked over cakes and tea,
and both of you knew you were going to do
what the cuttlefish do in the sea.

They have a faceful of feelers,
which gives them a worried air
and their bodies are bags of ocean,
with a skirt all round to steer.

They know how to change colour
and they know how to make love.
The female trembles underneath,
the male trembles above.

He's passed her a gobbet of pearl drops.
She's glued her eggs to a weed.
They swam off side by side and quietly died,
having planted the cuttlefish seed.

And you know that if you have to
there's a quiet hotel you can go
where you can tremble on top of her
and she can tremble below.

She has a W and an H
and a Y between her legs.
When you've read it all night you may answer it right –
you do it because of the eggs.

If you really really had to,
you would do it till you were both dead –
leave the embryo, like the cuttlefish do,
glued to the foot of the bed.

K. M. DERSLEY
MYTHICAL LIFELINES

Tony harks back all the time to the days
when we were not only gunslingers together but
men of the keyboard and quill.
As if we knew White's or the Diogenes Club
which we didn't, though I suppose
it wasn't dissimilar.

He harks back to when Dickens was presenting
his Pickwick effusions in 32-page
gobbets at sixpence each.

Lavender hair oil, was it, along with the
cufflinks? Did we think we'd go out and chat
with Haggard and Kipling, ol' Rudyard & Rider?
Was it Arnold Bennettville? Or more like the
domain of Frank Richards?
Tony sees the repercussions today on the keyboard
of the clever Compaq.

We knew the juiciness of Henry Miller's Clichy streets
without budging from Suffolk. We reckoned.

Oh yes, we go way back, even to where
Roddenberry beat out treatments about the Enterprise
on a battered electric. Or his earlier
efforts for *Have Gun, Will Travel*.

The fact is, it's an ongoing
fantasia. Tony even got
at a second hand shop
the same model, a Good Companion,
used by the creator of Noddy
like a divine
threshing machine.

BRIAN HENRY
UR-HAMLET

My uncle wagered against future earnings,
my mother forsaken to *seethe* and *forsooth*,
I pause to choose the route of my clamber,
agoggle at the sun's sudden entry.

My mother, forsaken, seethes and, forsooth,
picks the card that spells spoils and lesions,
a goggle to the sun's sudden entry.
Stowage for topple's reduction of sound,

pick the card that spells spoils and lesions!
Entrance to interference borne by command,
stowage for topple's reduction of sound,
tufts of broken bristles strafe down.

Entrance to interference born, by command
the knocker in my skull deflates me,
tufts of broken bristles strafe down,
my other's ambition an epoxy of sweat.

The knocker in my skull deflates me
and spit weds matter to water, resounds,
my other's ambition an epoxy of sweat
when displayed before a fickle crowd.

And spit – *Wed matter to water* – resounds,
my answer to this and all stern warnings
when displayed before a fickle crowd
(no answer truly, for circuit makes me certain).

My answer to this and all stern warnings
is the bestowal of bread to those who need the dark-
(no answer truly, for circuit makes me certain)
ness of dampness to hollow them out, lung by heart.

Is the bestowal of bread to those who need the dark
initiative taken nobler than that forgotten-
ness of dampness? To hollow them out, lung and heart,
these tergiversations are their own reasons.

Initiative taken nobler than that forgotten,
it ends, my other, for whose final number
these tergiversations are their own reasons.
Now can be heard to him that listens.

It ends, my other, whose final number
I pause to choose. The route of my clamber
now can be heard to him that listens,
my uncle wagered against future yearnings.

BOB KAVEN

MRS. WILSON'S DECLINING YEARS

Her brownstone townhouse offered a realtor's
       Fine view of Boston Harbor.
Behind her spacious bay windows, antic

Parrots frisked and capered in a flutter;
       With a compressed energy,
She cut her etchings onto copper plates.

Every autumn, through her declining years,
       She could feel God's stiff judgment
Brace Beacon Hill like liquid nitrogen.

Upstairs, a shriek of Northern winter light
       Poured, loud as rage, past windows
Of her attic, while edema clamped wrists

And ankles of both tourists and the poor.
       All moist surfaces adhered.
Each afternoon she sketched pale green palm fronds

With her steel nibs. Her monkey grandchildren
       Dangled from her skirt, loving
Her tricks –, how she pulled two dozen needles,

Strung on thread, from her mouth, like Houdini.
       While the children slept, florists
Renewed the house with roses. Silky light

Covered her floors in dreamy yellow sheets.
        The grandchildren sat for hours
In the sun room, the windows speckled with

Dried salt. They spent enormous time teaching
        The peculiar parrots speech.
Grandmother was delighted. The parrots

Displayed their eccentric wit like critics,
        Trilling their brittle complaints
In some language almost clear as English.

SARAH WARDLE
THE CLOSE

Where do they live, the sounds of other people,
the boy who plays his trumpet out of key,
the woman talking at her kitchen table,
the snatch of a tennis match on T.V.,

the sprinkler on a lawn, set to stop and go,
the dog that barks whenever it is bored,
the music from a curtained upstairs window,
the wood pigeon which plays its stuck record?

Where do they live, in or outside you?
You ask till you no longer want to know,
because you can hear your own footsteps too,
and the silence of your shadow on the road.

Fig on the Tyne

ADAM THORPE ON THE SELF-STYLED ANTI-LAUREATE

TONY HARRISON

Laureate's Block and Other Poems

Penguin, £7.99
ISBN 0 140 5 8923 6

THE TITLE POEM of this collection scuppered whatever chance Tony Harrison had of receiving the Laureateship, honouring (and implicitly identifying with) Thomas Gray's rejection of the post two centuries earlier. Written, like Gray's *Elegy* and Harrison's own *v.* (1985), in five-beat quatrains, using the same simple rhyme-scheme *abab*, its form is ideal for the kind of rueful punning humour Harrison excels in – here, the vocabulary of poetry-speak serves a new and lugubrious turn:

> No doubt inspired by the lunchtime news
> the salesman, passing volumes by myself,
> was selecting all the second-hand Ted Hughes
> to move to the window from the poetry shelf

Derek Attridge, in *The Rhythms of English Poetry*, has pointed out the peculiar quality of this form: "the five-beat line is brought back to the lyrical symmetries from which it is more usually the means of escape... to create a meditation free from the rough rhythms – and, one might add, the rough emotions – of real speech". It is one of the ironies of Harrison's work that, despite his vigorous use of a northern vernacular, he rarely lets us hear it in its natural, flexible, "spoken" form (as even Lawrence's exultant free verse does): it is always in the service of the strongly rhythmical (and rhyming) tradition of popular verse, drama and song. Blank verse is for the "poncy" sophisticates – those with an ear sufficiently attuned to recognise its limitless subtleties and still call it poetry: when he does forego rhyme, as here in 'Passer' (mourning Socialism's ruins), it is in the service of an Anglo-Saxon/Peter Reading pastiche, feverishly alliterated:

> But soaks' slop's sustaining to the spuggy survivor;
> the spuggy picks over the piss-artist's spew,
> the *passer* picks over the piss-artist's puke
> unsqueamish in Corfu at squid-rings in sick slosh...

As a political satirist, Harrison's models are the Latin poets and their eighteenth-century imitators – Pope, Dryden, Charles Churchill, the savage intelligibility of Swift. He is as much of a pessimist as the typical Augustan, struggling to believe in the corrective power of his art, Dryden's "amendment of Vices". The chief Vice, for Harrison, is class oppression; the insistent couplets continue to chime the knell of 'RP' – "took/suck", "but/soot", "full/skull" – but in a world where social legitimacy is now measured not so much in birth and voice as in wealth. Perhaps this is the reason why, despite its *Militant*-style cover, the latest collection offers more plangency than pugnaciousness. Rochester claimed that a man "could not write with life, unless he were heated with Revenge, for to make a Satire without Resentments... was as if a man would in cold blood cut men's throats, who had never offended him". In contrast to, say, the scourging eighteenth-century pen of Peter Pindar, Harrison's attacks on public figures are fleeting – the awkward "toadies like Di-deifying Motion" and the feeble "up yours to Tony Blair" being about the extent of it here. The insinuation, at the end of 'A Celebratory Ode on the Abdication of King Charles III', that "Laureate Hughes" would write a royal paean for the sake of a lordship, is suitably malicious, but in the title poem (written "the day / that Ted Hughes, sadly, [*sic*] died"), the late target has become the much chummier "Ted".

The Gulf War poems of 1992 lashed out in knotted intricacies, while their republican successors have been given too much slack. Perhaps they've been left behind by the inflammatory, complex intensities of rap, to whose strict rhythm and rhyme they bear some relation and in which the contemporary "dispossessed" find ear and tongue. Certainly, the mere fact that poems in a liberal newspaper can earn the "notorious" soubriquet by mildly binning the monarchy and its versifying "rat-catcher", suggests the task is far too easy. As Harrison himself points out, the post is one "Gray wouldn't credit still exists": it holds poetry up to public ridicule, even in hands as grand as Hughes's. Any answering ridicule has to be mercilessly sharp: as Dryden put it, "there is still a vast difference betwixt the slovenly Butchering of a Man, and the fineness of a stroak that separates the Head from the Body, and leaves it standing in its place".

When the grand old Duke of Marlborough died, Swift didn't blanch: "This world he cumber'd long enough: / He burnt his candle to the snuff; / And that's the reason, some folks think. / He left behind so great a stink". There is little of this bitter, brutal wit in *Laureate's Block*: much more prevalent is what Dryden's contemporaries would have called (not disapprovingly) 'Sentiments of Heart'. In the end, as with the "controversial" *v.*, what is much more interesting about the title poem is its personal braiding of place, mood and biography. The poet is in Stratford, his lover is playing Queen Elizabeth in *Richard III*, he buys a four-volume Gray and reads it in bed, she leaves the pretend play of royalty and murder and they make love: both poem and Gray's volume slide off the bed. The joke about Queen Elizabeth being "under the duvet" with him belongs to humour, not wit a distinction crucial to satire and its demise as understood by eighteenth century commentators. The political thread is submerged and, I would say, disarmed by this sentimental history: we can only take both genres on board in an implicit recognition of satire's defeat.

It seems that, having triumphantly occupied "your lousy leasehold Poetry" over the last thirty years, Harrison's diatonic drum-beat has lost its angry weight. There is no "your" any more. His resentments – famously crystallised in his English teacher's mockery of his "barbarian" accent – no longer seem to knuckle up behind his verse or brawl behind the gauze of his habitual tight form. Even the elegies to his parents in this book are celebratory of their union, rubbing each others' backs with lumbago balm or making grog together: 'Mouthfuls', which resurrects his father's tongue (both taste and sound) in his own, is reconciliatory. There is no agonised rebuff in this nostalgia, as

with their remarkable predecessors.

This softening is as much philosophical as emotional: 'Fruitility', a complex retake on the wonderfully sensuous 'A Kumquat for John Keats', bobs along on its papaya-fuelled way through mad or dying friends' miseries, AIDS victims, homeless wrecks in the New York street below, memories of wartime poverty. In mood it reminded me, not of the fig-sucking Lawrence, but of the New York poet Frank O'Hara, if formally far from O'Hara's chattering riffs. Life is futile, but full of sweet fruit – the message of the earlier poem, but whose lyrical profundity is a dim echo here: the delightful neologism is illustrated, not plumbed. His mother's "wartime wisdom" – embracing "good and grotty with sweet grace" – is merely saccharine after the displayed pain: I preferred it when we heard her bottom teeth click in the silences of those tense childhood teas in Leeds.

The finest poem in the book, 'Rice-Paper Man', faces, not backwards to origins, but forwards to a future for the poet's mentally-ill son. In desperately searching for a "cure" in a Spanish church or Japanese temple, Harrison characteristically weaves in a host of references, from Pol Pot to bull-fighting, and turns the poem into its own troubling act of faith:

You may have other props but this is mine.
Follow me down this stairway, line by line,
solidarity in darkness, writer/reader,
tu mi segui, e io sàro tua guida.

Despite its range of references, the poem is almost painfully simple in its diction. Its obsessive repetitions (not just phrases – we see him light the candle or scribble the message on the rice-paper figure over and over again, as in a film) create internal refrains that mirror Dante's circles of Hell and the spirals of his son's paranoia, as well as mimicking the poet's "drive to shape / that throws up no solutions nor escape" – explicitly blamed for his son's condition. This is Harrison's hallmark: to beat out the meaning on a form uncannily imitative, despite its tight dimensions, not of "real speech" but of the underlying patterns and pressures of thought and emotion. His real innovation was to have dusted off forms long relegated to light verse and weight them with his own trauma: the

politics was always personal, the conflict as much in the heart as beyond. That heart now threatens, like the ripe fig he grows on the Tyne, to overwhelm his work with sweetness.

You can order this book POST-FREE from the PBS at £7.99. See p.85 for details.

Sparks of the Smithy

by Paul Groves

DENNIS O'DRISCOLL
Weather Permitting
Anvil, £7.95
ISBN 0 85646315 9

THIS POETRY BOOK Society Recommendation is the fifth collection by a forty-six-year-old Irish Customs official. For those who know the name but have not read the poet a treat lies in store. Throughout three sections containing thirty-two poems one hears a civilised, undemonstrative voice and encounters a keen intelligence which is difficult to resist. Seamus Heaney scholars will doubtless discover the Great Man's influence among these pages, but essentially O'Driscoll is his own person. Although one finds such locations as "a hill farm scoured / by yard light" ('Four Destinations') which echo the Nobel laureate's "the lamplit / slabs of a yard" ('The Last Mummer') it is unhelpful to hunt for parallels.

O'Driscoll writes from a religious background, from "faith as firm as mine was then". Doubt seems to have intruded. 'Churchyard View: The New Estate', which constitutes the whole of Part Two, does not glow with religionist zeal but depicts its subject with melancholy accuracy. Most poets have written about death, few as successfully as here. O'Driscoll draws strength from reticence; his cadences have more power packed into them than appearances suggest, like a matchbox of plutonium. In the assiduously-end-stopped 'The Victim' his tone inhabits a hinterland of unrelieved bleakness.

He is no stranger to puns. They enrich the language rather than tickle the ribs. Consider not holding a "party" at the tennis club hall but a "bash". Witness a "crane, throwing its weight around" (meaning a demolition ball). Watch "Burning candles toast / a corner of the church", which sounds calorific but is "*To your good health, / happiness, success*", a different toasting entirely. Savour the delicious ambiguity of "Wind bellows. Stars hiss like smithy sparks". Mostly the playfulness is kept in check. The world contains too much pain to allow levity to blossom. The overall tone is nostalgic, summed up by the book's borrowed last line: *A caged bird pines for its first forest, a salmon thirsts for its stream.*

His parents are no longer alive, yet in part VII of 'Family Album' they "have enough flesh left / to shoot a glance / at one another's eyes". Admittedly the poet is dreaming, though the way "my father clasps / my mother's hand" is real enough. Time and again O'Driscoll speaks of the human condition with unsentimental empathy. Almost in spite of himself, he is on the side of life: in 'Snail's Pace' he could stamp on the vulnerable mollusc, or "nip inside / for salt to liquidate it" but lets "it go about its sluggish routines in the end". We, too, have our routines, vividly delineated in '9. A.M.', which lists what happens in an average city at that hour – a good exercise to set a creative writing class. It is a safe bet no student would surpass this perceptive effort.

The book's strengths are so numerous that reservations sound like quibbling. Once in a while the writer's dispassionate orderliness can prompt one to long for a few torrid divulgences; the dedication – to "JULIE through thick and thin" – tempts one to expect the occasional emotional roller-coaster ride. It is not to be. Yet when he does essay lushness, as in section III of the title poem – "after

Leopardi", the result can be too rich against his pervasive quiet sardonicism. 'Breviary''s five poems could be omitted: they are too short to say anything of significance. Even so, 'Departures', the first of them, would be lost with some regret. Lines can be so short that space invades the page: 'To Love' has thirty-five lines, fourteen of which are three words long. And in 'Towards a Cesare Pavese Title' each of its fourteen lines contains "death", while all but the last contain "eye[s]": such repetition is usually something of a gamble.

Generally, what the reader will want of O'Driscoll is more of the same. In 'Life Cycle in memory of George Mackay Brown' we get twelve three-line stanzas, one for each month. This is part of May: "Scissors-tailed swallows cut the tape, declare summer open. / A stray daddy-long-legs, unsteady on its feet as a new foal". Unlike Yeats's "long-legged fly upon the stream" O'Driscoll's mind does not move upon silence, it ruminates on experience with alacrity, humility, and an unwillingness to pontificate. His talent – which could equally grace a novel – should stand the test of time.

You can order this book POST-FREE from the PBS at £7.95. See p.85 for details.

Feeling as Knowledge

by John Burnside

PAULINE STAINER

Parable Island

Bloodaxe £7.95
ISBN 1 85224 501 8

PENELOPE SHUTTLE

A Leaf Out Of His Book

Carcanet £7.95
ISBN 1 90303900 2

Poems that spring out fully armed; and those that are the result of artisan care. The contrived poem, workmanship; a sense of achievement and pride of craft; but the pure inspiration flow leaves one with a sense of gratitude and wonder, and no sense of "I did it" That level of mind – the cool water – not intellect and not – (as romantics and after have confusingly thought) fantasy-dream world or unconscious.

THUS GARY SNYDER, considering the techniques and practices of poetry in his seminal work, Earth House Hold. It is a view of inspiration which has not, perhaps, caught on in British poetry, with its insistence on anecdote, workmanship and deliberate irony; nevertheless, in spite of its acknowledged legislators, the church of poetry appears broad enough to include those who might be described as working in Snyder's "inspired" mode, (as long as we are able to set aside the conventional / reductionist modes of thinking, and see inspiration, or intuition, entirely as an extra-sensory skill which we cannot altogether explain). By reductionist, I mean to indicate an apparently rational, but really rather simplistic mode of thinking about the world which is most commonly mistaken for science in everyday parlance, and for objectivity in art. As Paul Virilio says, in *The Aesthetics of Disappearance* (speaking of what he calls "basic research"):

> We in turn have come to know this frozenness, a veritable plague of collective conformity, and if it's now in fashion to criticize methodological reason, until now we have had almost no works addressing the repression of feeling in science in a group of scientists under its influence.

Against this (pseudo-)scientific repression of "feeling", (or intuition), Virilio sets the work of the parapsychologists, whose aim it is to "put in question the sensorial categories", as well as those thinkers and artists for whom intuition is a visible aspect of the creative process. For example, he cites Magritte, speaking in 1960: "I never show bizarre or strange objects in my pictures...they are always familiar things... .gathered and transformed in such a way that we're made to think that *there's something else of an unfamiliar nature that appears at the same time as familiar things*" [Virilio's italics].

One might say that a poetry has evolved in England in which the only permissible feeling – in this sense of "feeling as knowledge" – is a kind of wry self-consciousness (as opposed to self-aware-ness), which naturally results in an embarrassment from which the only escape is an emphatic irony. Against self-consciousness, however, we might posit awareness, a sense characteristic of those poets (and other artists) who share Snyder's view of the work.

Penelope Shuttle, as both thinker and poet, seems to me exemplary in her use of the intuitive faculty: a self-forgetful procedure for the renewal of awareness which one might describe as the making of leaps, rather than the taking of "logical" steps, or what Virilio, discussing Proust, calls "the Sophist idea of *apate,* the suddenness of this possible entry into another logic". Thus, in the beautiful 'A Sleeve's Mood', we enter into a logic which works by intuition, and has nothing at all to do with Romanticism:

> A sleeve's mood, like a leaf
> or lip guarding the memoir,
> or a pendulum
> that takes a nap, or smiles,
> as it tours its veils,
> its forgery books, its handles
> that froth up...

Shuttle often works with dream imagery, but this never entails a search for easy surrealism, or the construction of a decorative device. Instead, a procedure is evident, by which the poem seeks, not explanation, but understanding. The principle is delightfully encapsulated in the poem 'In All Weathers':

> A dream cannot procure you
> wealth in the world
>
> but it has a gilt-edged tongue,
> is an arguer of luminous cunning,
>
> shares out its riches
> like any friend sharing sorrows
> in all weathers.

By contrast, Pauline Stainer's world is one in which time and space are seen to possess the same logic as the kind of dream from which Dostoevski's Dmitri awakes, in *The Brothers Karamazov,* with a cry of understanding (though his circumstances are far beyond either explanation or ordinary resolu-tion). Time and again, we shift into a new logic, an

awareness of the "unfamiliar nature that appears at the same time as familiar things" which might have been witnessed "when Orpheus played". Stainer's entire *oeuvre* is typified, not only by inspiration (in Snyder's sense), but also by a far from ascetic rigour: she is as concerned with language as any other poet, but she is also interested in how poetry may "become again / prologue to the whole" (reminis-cent, in this usage, of what Heidegger calls "projec-tive saying"). Thus, the title of this new collection is more than a clue to its reading (many of the poems are set in the Orkneys, where Stainer was then living), it is a statement of poetic intent. Against the casual anecdote (casual, that is, in the sense of 'lack-ing in tension') which might be seen as the predom-inant fashion, she sets the more ambiguous, multivalent and intuitive power of parable. It might be said that a story is a story – that we make of it what we will; here, the parable (or the parable-poem) invokes a reality which, though invisible to the usual senses, governs our lives at the most funda-mental levels. Thus, in Parable Island, Stainer returns, often, to the question of time, or rather, durée:

> passerines,
> weightless after migration –
> magnetic particles
> of iron oxide
> in their retinas –
> spirits fired with blood
>
> as on St Kilda,
> where if you put your ear
> to the carbon-dating,
> you hear the wrens
> settle like small rain
> on the tree rings.
>   ('St Brendan's birds')

Inspired, or intuited, the apprehension of the real in the work of both these poets, is something for which we must be grateful. Poetry like this is essential to our seeing of the "invisible which is real", it is also a gift, in the fullest sense of the word. "It's a metaphysical act", Stainer says, of "Finding the right blue for the waterfall"; an act which, in itself, is fundamental to the diurnal ceremony of being in the world.

You can order these books POST-FREE from the PBS.
See p.85 for details.

Her Life Awake

by John Kinsella

JO SHAPCOTT

Her Book

Faber, £8.99
isbn 0 571 20183 0

JO SHAPCOTT IS doing no less than rewriting the English poetic canon – challenging sources, verse structure, and the primacy of the patriarchal voice. Her "class" or social milieu is female in a world of mass media, where all language is negotiated through male power structures; her verse undoes this and creates an alternative. It is critical and self-aware, amusing and cutting. It is enjoyable to read and can needle you long after it's left.

Shapcott has a brilliant sense of how the line can be played against to enhance meaning, to make a point about tone and speed by turning before we expect her to. Her use of mythology, "tradition" and convention in the construction of histories is powerful. Her ability to use "voice" versatile. Her gender play on anthropomorphics stylish, as in 'Cheetah Run': "I whisper, 'I'm coming baby', to the distant hare / though my head's turned the full 180 degrees away".

This is a poetry alive with information – a virtual stage alive with voices heard over the static of media propaganda. For Shapcott, the language of popular culture is vivid and ever-present and subverting notions of the past. Which is not to deny the presence of history, but rather to reevaluate it in the light of change. Ironic, witty and alive, she can construct personae at will, always to a political end. She can write about what it means to be English

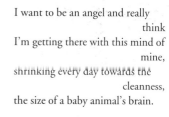

with both intense authenticity and subjectivity, and at the same time critical distance. This is a significant achievement – the separation of powers, of language and social truth, is difficult, if not impossible. Shapcott at least highlights the threads. Like all great satirists, she is both part of the culture she is analysing, and able to step – momentarily – outside it.

Shapcott's use of "regular" speech and the colloquial is equally impressive. *Her Book* is a "compendium" of Shapcott's three published books, *Electroplating the Baby*, *Phrase Book*, and *My Life Asleep*. It isn't a large *oeuvre*, but then there is no excess. Shapcott anticipates her critics at every turn. She knows what she is up against. She will be attacked for what she does. The conflation of poetry, sexism, language, the media and even economics is brilliantly conveyed in her well-known "Mad Cow" poems – poems of female fetishisation. We read in 'The Mad Cow in Love':

I want to be an angel and really
                                    think
I'm getting there with this mind of
                                    mine,
shrinking every day towards the
                                    cleanness,
the size of a baby animal's brain.

The world is vivid for Shapcott – there are metamorphoses and transformations, the empowerment and freedom of the body are one. Nothing is Manichaean. In 'Her Lover's Ear' –

I was glad to see you:
I thought I might know in my
                                    human life
how to touch you lightly
after this rehearsal as a piece of dust.

A small neat poem that might be read as a mini *ars-poetica* is 'Watching Medusa', bearing in mind Cixous' essay 'The Laugh of the Medusa', in which we read: "You only have to look at the Medusa straight on to see her. And she's not deadly. She's beautiful and she's laughing". It's another poem from the ironic pages of the Shapcott gender bestiary. Here's the poem in full; form-wise it is not especially characteristic of Shapcott, but as she's such a versatile, formally dynamic poet it is impossible to say any specific poem is characteristic.

Watching Medusa

Struck dumb when I saw
her scalp begin to stir,

saw the little eyes slide
like drops through her hair,

saw them look back at me
kindly and fluid

as a bunch of lovers.
I cannot speak or move

in case I do wrong to her and
close the sweet hissing mouths

Here we have a challenge to the mythologies of patriarchy. The Medusa is not even "terrifyingly" beautiful – just full of her own inner creative beauty. In this poem the "muse" is "rescued" – is reclaimed from the male poet. The male can't take this this because by his own definition he will turn to stare – rendered incapable, This is a sleight-of-hand poetically, but entirely honest thematically. The rules have changed. And whose rules were they in the first place? Shapcott is a poet for whom Tom and Jerry can be acting out a storyline in England – "swished my axe at Jerry, belted after him / into the Bloody Tower, my back legs / circling like windmills in a gale..." – the barriers between the allowable and the forbidden are broken. Nothing is sacred. She is English, but could almost be "post-colonial" in her irreverence. And in a monarchy, history is inviolable – but not for Shapcott. This is political poetry. The centre doesn't hold, and she's here to tell us about it.

In an early poem like 'With the Big Tray', Shapcott casually deconstructs the traditional male "artist's" gaze. The "nude descending the staircase" motif is inverted –

With the big tray
Hilary had to mind the tea service
at each end of the long march
up the staircase (those places
by the newel posts where her hips
had to angle and re-angle
at the new levels)...

This is about what's available to the gaze – especially via "tradition", and especially the false liberation of seeing of modern nude art. To upset the portrait within the *mise-en-scène* – the taboo is deployed and broken:

The sun constructed an avenue
to the bedside table
and now the housefly played
boomerang in and out of the light.
Hilary surprised herself by breaking wind.
Secretly, her large smell
made her feel real and salty
as a merchant adventurer...

The gender play here is deft and unrelenting. Some years back the Australian comedian Andrew Denton made a joke that for a man to live as a woman he might need "lessons in fart suppression" – like custody of the eyes, women keeping their metaphysical eyebeams to themselves.

One of Shapcott's best-known poems, 'Phrase Book', demonstrates her language play at its most damaging and smart. The tensions between the body and language, the domestic and public, the woman seen as the "aside" of war, despite the physical consequences. A poem about the Gulf War and the use of the language of propaganda in the contemporary media-savvy international military environment, and specifically the language of English-speaking pilots in action. This is the "truth" on the screens, in the living room. It is a brilliant disabling of imperialism and text:

... This is my own front room

where I'm lost in the action, live from a war,
on screen. I am an Englishwoman, I don't understand you...

It's also a bizarre "love" poem, of sorts, or a poem of deathly consummation between the viewer and the screen images and their peculiar language.

A shorter version of this piece appeared in the *Observer*.

You can order this book POST-FREE from the PBS at £8.99. See p.85 for details.

GRETA STODDART
THE CROSSING

Like a diver come to the end of the board
I stall a moment, hinging at the kerb
when something I'd taken for lost returns:
the image of our lady stood on the corner,
her white plastic coat aglow in the rain,
the way she never smiled spoke but could,
with the raising of one blistered hand,
bring to heel those hundreds of men.
And how once she'd paved the way for us
to walk, hand in hand and without fear,
for the seconds it took to cross we felt ourselves
to be centre-stage before the town
who sat, stilled and doleful in their seats.
And always when we passed we'd glance up
at her chins, gently carved and receding
as she stood surveying her becalmed sea.

Once, swinging the corner I froze — oh!
there she goes waddling away in a blue cape,
unleashing her see-through bonnet to the wind! —
leaving me stranded, wild-eyed,
a hand to the prayer bubbling up in my mouth.
If only I'd known of a time like now when,
in the dark and blurry wave of a London rush-hour,
I can step out and stay, inviolable as in a dream,
treading water between the glittering streams.

NEWS/COMMENT

POETRY'S BEST SELLERS

In modern publishing sometimes a single book can open up a new genre. A demand is shown to exist by the freak best-seller and further best-sellers duly follow. The classic example was the emergence of SAS books following Andy McNab's *Bravo Two Zero*. Dava Sobel's *Longitude,* although it could be classified under an already established sector, popular science, seems to belong to a sub-class all of its own. It might seem strange that the ancient art of poetry should be re-invented as a bookshop genre in this way but that is what seems to have happened. Two kinds of book are behind this movement.

The first is anthologies, begun by *Poems on the Underground* and then developed by the BBC in its *Nation's Favourite* series. This is now such a banker that even *The Nation's Favourite 20th Century Poems*, published three years after its poll because at the time it was considered uncommercial, has joined the ranks of the best-sellers. The other category was spawned by a single book, Ted Hughes's *Birthday Letters*. The genre could be called larger-than-life personality poetry. Seamus Heaney's *Beowulf* is clearly selling largely on its universally acknowledged merits, but the benign spin-off from *Birthday Letters* is undeniable. The latest beneficiary of this factor is Carol Ann Duffy's *The World's Wife*, with Simon Armitage's *Killing Time* bidding to join them. Heaney, Hughes, Duffy and Armitage are all represented, of course, in *The Nation's Favourite 20th Century Poems* and here is where the convergence between these books and the anthologies emerges. The more poets who become established as personalities, the more names readers will recognise in anthologies of twentieth-century poetry, and the more such anthologies are sold, the more individual poets included in them will start to gain readers.

A beachhead has thus been established, that will change poetry publishing from the little cottage industry it has been for so long. The analogy here is with football, with a two-tier system emerging: a premier league of best-selling poets and the rest probably selling somewhat fewer books than they did before the boom. Every now and then a poet will be promoted into the premier league. Carol Ann Duffy has recently echoed this magazine in saying that "the slim volume culture must change". It seems to be happening.

TOP OF THE IRISH POEMS

Question: What is the best poem ever written by an Irish poet?
Answer: 'The Lake Isle of Innisfree'.
Question: Who says so?
Answer: Readers of the *Irish Times* responding to a request from that paper and *Poetry Ireland* to pick their three favourite poems. The results were printed in the *Irish Times* on the eve of the millennium and are available on their website at www.ireland.com.

What W. B. Yeats would have made of his early lyric reaching the number 1 spot on Top of The Poems is anyone's guess, but it's said that he never recovered from a visit to the Royal Albert Hall where he endured the sound of thousands of boy scouts reciting the poem in unison. Did he arise and go then? He probably endorsed the title of the number two poem: 'He Wishes for the Cloths of Heaven'. Like the Beatles, he ends up with six poems in the top ten. At Yeats, you get much more.

And what would Seamus Heaney think of coming in at number three with 'Mid Term Break'. The poem may be clever, emotional, and nostalgic, but it is far from being the best a Mossbawn man can do. However, Heaney has some consolation offered by *Poetry Ireland*'s Theo Dorgan's method of assessment. Based on the number of poems nominated by readers, famous Seamus is given the accolade of Ireland's number one poet, pushing Yeats into second place. What then, sang Yeats's ghost, what then?

There is no doubt that this list of the top 100 poems is interesting (more so than the top 10 poets) but only significant if you are someone for whom Guinness means books of records and not pints of plain. (Flann O'Brien's old chestnut comes in at number 46.) The results of this poll have as much bearing on contemporary Irish poetry as an MRBI poll (also beloved of the *Irish Times*) has on contemporary Irish politics.

Imagine a list, any list, of Irish poems that has nothing by Michael Longley, nothing by Richard Murphy, nothing by Nuala Ní Dhomhnaill and nothing by Ciaran Carson. And from an earlier generation, there is nothing by John Synge, nothing by James Stephens, nothing by Oliver St. John Gogarty and nothing by Samuel Beckett. Nor is there any selection from Brendan Kennelly; at least two of his book-length epic poems, 'Cromwell' and 'The Book of Judas', should have made the cut. Perhaps he will end up endorsing the title of his third epic, 'Poetry, My Arse'.

What is there is a "preponderance of poems learned in school". Theo Dorgan gives a benign interpretation: "well, that's interesting in itself; it suggests, doesn't it, that there's something to be said for rote learning?" It does not. What it suggests is that many readers who fill in surveys could not be bothered going beyond what they picked up in school. Poetry may, like Guinness, be good for you, but not good enough to pursue unaided. Who, having read Thomas Kinsella, would pick 'Mirror in February' and 'Another September'? Only some-one who studied *Soundings*, the Leaving Certificate English textbook which has been required reading for all 15- to 18-year old students in Ireland for the past 30 years and which as a result, is probably the best-selling poetry book in Ireland in the twentieth century. How else account for the fact that Austin Clarke has three poems in the top 100, the three from *Soundings*? Even Patrick Kavanagh, who has a dozen poems chosen, sees ten of them come from the school anthologies. Have poems, will travel.

Maybe, as Theo Dorgan says, these are "the 100 Irish poems the people of Ireland care most about and have taken to their hearts" or maybe "the people of Ireland", all 3,000 of them who voted (and is there a bit of vote-rigging in eightieth position which has nineteen entries?) rarely read poetry after schooldays end and life begins in earnest. As always, the standing army of Irish poets is far more numer-ous than the sitting partisans of Irish poetry readers.

The poem that comes last on the list (number 100) is John Montague's delicate, delightful love lyric, 'All Legendary Obstacles'. Where it should be on the list is a matter for criticism but hardly a crit-ical matter. But it is a far better poem, and Montague is a far better poet, than many of those included above him. And this listless literary list is merely an obstacle to recognising that fact.
Conor Kelly

NET VERSE

Able Muse at **http://www.ablemuse.com/** is a new review of metrical poetry edited from California (though where they come from seems to matter less and less with online magazines). The first issue features good work from featured poet Beth Houston, an interesting essay on the Sonnet in the 20th century, more poetry and light verse. It also has some excellent artwork. A neat touch is the direct link to Amazon for books by featured poets.

Another newish journal, now on its second issue

is *slope*. I probably don't have to tell you more about it than that it's at **http://www.slope.org/** and that the issue features names like William Oxley, Peter Finch, John Kinsella, and Sheila Murphy, to convince you it's worth a visit.

Poetry London at **http://www.poetrylondon. co.uk/** is a taster for the print magazine, but has quite a bit of up-to-date news and information. What they're hoping for, of course, is that the site will whet your appetite just enough to make you go out and buy the full paper version.

Paul Deane is passionate that alliterative and accentual poetry still has a place in the 21st century, and he makes an excellent case at his interesting *Forgotten Ground Regained* site at **http://www. jps.net/pdeane/fgr/**. He has sample poems, essays and explanations, and the site is an valuable resource, even if you don't feel as strongly as he does.

Jane Dorner's new book *The Internet: A Writer's Guide* is a much needed survey of and introduction to what the Internet has to offer. The accompany-ing website at **http://www.internetwriter.co.uk/** serves a double purpose. As well as providing the contents and some extracts, there's a password protected part of the site with links to all 800 or so websites mentioned in the book. Buy the book and you get the password, which saves you a lot of typing.

If there's a site that should be mentioned here, let me know at **peter@hphoward.demon.co.uk**

PBS EXCLUSIVE BOOK SUPPLY SERVICE

We apologise for the incorrect phone number given in the last issue – the new style number attracted an extra digit en route from the PBS to the Poetry Society. The correct number is: 0208 870 8403 between 9.30am and 5.30pm Mon-Fri. Readers of *Poetry Review* can receive most of the books featured in the magazine post-free from the PBS by this service. If your local bookshop's idea of a poetry section is a shelf of Keats *Collected* and two tatty copies of *The Waste Land* this is what you've been waiting for! Call to make your order, quoting "*Poetry Review*". All major credit/debit cards accepted, including Switch.

LETTERS

HAUGHTY MUDDLE

Dear Peter,

Christopher Ricks's *Oxford Book of English Verse* is indeed vulnerable, sometimes questionable in its decisions, omissions, and inclusions. But it is not, I think, the kind of haughty muddle which William Scammell makes it out to be in his review (Vol. 89 No. 4, p45).

In particular, Scammell ignores two points which Ricks states in his Introduction. First, there is the importance given to verse translation, from Golding's Ovid, Chapman's Homer and Milton's Horace to Elaine Feinstein's Tsvetayeva and Heaney's Dante. (No doubt if it had appeared in time, space would have been made for something from Heaney's *Beowulf*.)

Well over forty of the pieces included are translations, and others are direct imitations from foreign languages. Ricks draws attention to this on p. xxxv, but Scammell takes no notice of it. Ricks's precursors, Quiller-Couch and Helen Gardner, lacked this ingredient.

Second, it's pointless for Scammell to itemise such omissions as Tony Harrison, Michael Longley, Derek Mahon, Douglas Dunn, Anne Stevenson, Fleur Adcock (some absences I too regret), when he fails to mention Ricks's decision, stated on p. xxxiv, writing about the "Historical Range" of the book. Ricks makes a crucial caveat: "Heaney, the only poet represented here who is younger than I am..." To make a birth-date of 1933 the cut-off point, and at the same time to include Heaney, may look arbitrary. But any maker of an anthology is an arbitrator – and, more pertinently in this case, Ricks clearly said what he had done.

Finally, what I would say about Ricks's decision to use my "magazine squib" (Scammell's phrase), 'On Consulting "Contemporary Poets of the English Language"', is that presumably he included it as a way of cutting the ground from under many reviewers' remarks if they chose to question his contemporary representation. Another reason might be that it puts the whole business of anthologising into perspective.

ANTHONY THWAITE

Low Tharston
Norfolk

OCCASIONALLY, A POET

Dear Peter Forbes,

Roddy Lumsden's review of *News That Stays News,* reveals typical metrocentric ignorance and snobbery when he refers, very patronisingly, to Phillip Whitfield as contributing one of "several poems not written by poets: occasional, emotional works which were largely inspired by being there". For his information, Phillip Whitfield wrote poetry throughout his long adult life. The KQBX press published a selection, *In Practice*, in 1993 and there are plans for a collected poems. His work as a general practitioner and paediatrician meant that he had little time for self-promotion, but it gave him a subject matter which his poems explored in a spirit of compassion and entirely without illusion. Gareth Owen, the poetry producer and presenter, wrote to me that he was "moved and delighted by many of the poems".

Miroslav Holub's poem 'Conversation with a poet' makes the point that a person is only a poet while writing a poem, and a new one at that, not while giving readings, reviewing books or scheming for grants, all activities which stop professional poets being poets for much of their time. On Holub's criterion, I suspect Phillip Whitfield was more of a poet, more of the time, than Roddy Lumsden.

Yours sincerely
MALCOLM POVEY
Bournemouth

Dear Editor,

I was mystified by Roddy Lumsden's claims about "poems not written by poets", and his attempt to dismiss them as "occasional, emotional works which were largely inspired by 'being there'". For a start, how do non-poets achieve a technique that can pass muster in a Faber anthology?

Then again, such comments surely require personal knowledge of – not sweeping assumptions about – the alleged non-poet's lack of other poetic output.

If Roddy Lumsden doesn't know about the rest of Phillip Whitfield's work, he's obviously not qualified to dismiss it in that way.

Had Hopkins had been on board the Deutschland, Tennyson taken part in the Charge of the Light Brigade, or Hardy survived the sinking of the Titanic, would Roddy think less of those occasional poems?

Probably not, because he enters a caveat for "the

compassionate, but removed stance of a skilled practitioner". So where does that leave war poets like Wilfred Owen, Isaac Rosenberg or Keith Douglas? Isn't their stance often emotional and inspired by "being there" – and are their poems the worse for that?

For my money, Whitfield's image (in the Belsen poem) of the "moving skeleton" gripping five grains of wheat in its palm is as powerful as the girl's photograph in 'Vergissmeinnicht'.

Oh, but then I was forgetting. Phillip Whitfield isn't a *poet*. Didn't get a Gregory or a book from Bloodaxe. Just spent half a century or more writing the best poems he was capable of producing. Sorry, that doesn't count. Not up there among the clouds of condescension that, far too often, hang over the pages of *Poetry Review*.

MARTIN BLYTH
Poole

PATOIS POEMS

Dear Sir
Paul Groves, in his review of *The Forward Book of Poetry* (Vol. 89 No. 4, p63), says my poem 'horse under water' leaves him 'uneasy, as if its creator – apparently a middle-class middle-aged white woman – were playing the ethnic-minority card it is politically correct these days to brandish. Nothing wrong with the ethnic minorities doing it, but for the rest of us to try is like appropriating their clothes".

I grew up in Jamaica and spoke as they did until I was sent back to England and the language was bashed out of me at school.

I never planned to write in dialect; the tongue came back to me, unlooked for, when I started to write poetry. I quickly discovered it was the most creative form for me to write in.

Jamaican culture remains the best and most exciting influence in my life although I have lived in many other places since I left.

David Dabydeen wrote to the *Guardian* last year saying: "She is a new voice from the Caribbean even though she spent only a few expatriate years there. What mattered was that the language lodged in her imagination and, therefore, became hers".

Yours sincerely
CAROLINE CARVER
Falmouth, Cornwall
P.S. Why is there a special stigma attached to being middle-aged?

BIOLOGY LESSONS

Dear Peter,
Somebody ought to tell "Categorical Imperative", the author of the untitled Classic Found Poem in the last *Poetry Review* (Vol. 89 No. 4, p17), that the poem did not work. It was a classic example of the emptiness of intellectual conceit.

Yours sincerely,
SEBASTIAN BARKER
London

SOME CONTRIBUTORS

John Agard was Poet in Residence at the BBC in 1999; his new collection, *Weblines*, is forthcoming from Bloodaxe.

Patience Agbabi is Poet in Residence at the Flamin' Eight Tattoo Shop; *Transformatrix* is forthcoming from Playback Press.

Fleur Adcock's Poetry Placement was in Kensington Gardens, Summer 1999. Her *Collected Poems* is just out from Bloodaxe.

Nicholas Baumfield is Director of MidNAG (Mid Northumberland Arts Group).

Bernardine Evaristo's placement was at The Museum of London in 1999. Her verse-novel *Lara* was published by Angela Royal in 1997.

Philip Gross had a placement in the Galleries, Shopping Centre, Bristol; his latest collection is *The Wasting Game (Bloodaxe, 1999)*.

Sophie Hannah's placement was at the Leeds Word Arena in June 1999. Her new novel is *Cordial and Corrosive* (Arrow, 2000).

Tobias Hill was Poet in Residence at London Zoo in 1998; his latest collection is *Zoo* (OUP).

Mimi Khalvati is currently Poet in Residence at the Royal Mail.

Roddy Lumsden was Poet in Residence with the record industry in 1999; his forthcoming collection, *The Book of Love* is a PBS Choice.

Ian McMillan was Poet in Residence on Northern Spirit trains in 1999; his latest collection is *I Found this Shirt,* Carcanet, 1999.

John Mole was Poet in the City in 1999; his latest collection is *Depending on the Light* (Peterloo).

Philip Parker is Editorial Manager at Royal Mail.

Peter Sansom was Poet in Residence at Marks and Spencer in 1998; his latest collection is *January* (Carcanet).

Mike Sharpe's pamphlet *Incomers* was published last year by Shoestring Press.

Matthew Sweeney was Poet in Residence at the National Library for the Blind; his new collection is *A Smell of Fish* (Cape, 2000).

Adam Taylor is a solicitor who attended John Mole's drop-in sessions in the City.

Jackie Wills is Poet in Residence in the Surrey Hills; *Powder Keg* (Arc, 1995) was a PBS Recommendation.

CORREX

Apologies to Ann Gray for misspelling her name in the last issue, page 73.

The last sentence of Elaine Feinstein's review of *In the Grip of Strange Thoughts* was amputated by Quark Xpress. It should read: "More dubious was the decision to exclude poets who died before 1990, so that there is nothing from two poet singers, Vyzotsky and Galich – both edgier and more subversive than Okudzhava – or the fine poet Boris Slutsky. Nevertheless, there is much here to relish".